Microwave Components

MODERN ELECTRICAL
STUDIES
A Series edited by
Professor G. D. SIMS
Head of Department of Electronics
University of Southampton

Microwave Components

P. A. MATTHEWS
B.Sc., Ph.D., C.Eng., M.I.E.E.

I. M. STEPHENSON
M.Sc., Ph.D., C.Eng., M.I.E.E., A.C.G.I.

*Lecturers in Electrical Engineering
at University College, London*

CHAPMAN AND HALL LTD.
11 NEW FETTER LANE, LONDON EC4

First published 1968
© *P. A. Matthews & I. M. Stephenson 1968*
Printed in England
by Butler & Tanner Ltd, Frome and London

Distribution in the U.S.A. by
Barnes & Noble, Inc.

Contents

v

Contents

Preface

over 60 years

Microwave techniques were first extensively developed nearly thirty years ago and cannot be regarded as new. However, in the last ten years there have been many changes in the field. Firstly, the use of microwave techniques has been greatly extended. In addition to the continued application in radar and navigation systems, there has been a tremendous growth in their use for communication systems, both as ground links and in satellite relays. Secondly the type of components used has also greatly changed. In the early days of microwaves, it was considered that only the waveguide could be used as a medium for transmission over short distances and for the construction of components. As a result of improved understanding of the problems involved and the availability of superior materials and constructional techniques, it has become possible to make many microwave devices using co-axial and stripline techniques. Furthermore the increasing use of microwave semiconductor devices has both increased the range of techniques possible and reduced the size and complexity of the equipment.

There are a number of books that already deal extremely adequately, and in considerable detail, with waveguide components so that our aim in writing this book has been to introduce the reader simultaneously to waveguide, co-axial and stripline techniques. In order to cover what is now a very extensive subject in a fairly short book, the treatment of individual devices is of necessity brief, and in many cases of a descriptive nature. However, we hope to have included sufficient theory in the first two chapters for the reader to be able to appreciate the principles involved.

One notable omission from this book is active devices. We felt that these devices, both thermionic and semiconductor, are so numerous and involve so many different physical principles that it would be impossible to deal with them adequately in one chapter. We have dealt briefly with passive semiconductor devices that are used in microwave systems.

A major development that we have covered is in microwave measurement techniques. The availability of electronically swept sources, sampling oscilloscopes and time domain reflectometry has revolutionized measurement techniques, which were hitherto limited to the laborious business of making endless readings on standing wave indicators. These advances have given the microwave engineer several new dimensions of vision and these in turn have resulted in improved components being developed.

The tremendous increase in the demands for communication, accelerated by such developments as colour television, data transmission and remote access to computers is already resulting in the search for systems with very wide bandwidths. In the near future, only microwave systems will be capable of handling this demand and microwave techniques will become of increasing importance.

P. A. MATTHEWS and I. M. STEPHENSON

London, 1968

CHAPTER 1

Introduction: Guided Waves

Most microwave systems are used to transmit information from one point to another. From many points of view free space, or air, is an ideal transmission medium as the attenuation of electromagnetic waves at wavelengths greater than a few centimetres is usually extremely small. There are several disadvantages to using an unbounded space as the propagating medium. As practical radiators do not produce an ideal plane wave, but a diverging beam, the receiving aerial may have to be enormous if it is to receive a reasonably large proportion of the transmitted power, and in practice almost all of the transmitted power is wasted. The space between the transmitter and receiver will often be the Earth's atmosphere and this will contain ionized gases, water vapour and raindrops which may alter the propagation characteristics. Free space transmission is subject also to interference and the transmission may be intercepted.

Whenever high transmission efficiency is required a guided wave system has to be used. The introduction of the guiding system introduces losses that are not normally present in the free space transmission. However these losses are more than offset by the fact that the waves are no longer divergent, but confined to a path of constant cross-section.

In this chapter we use the simple parallel plate transmission line to illustrate the two main types of guided wave propagation systems and to give an idea of the physical mechanism involved. The field equations for these simple systems have been derived but for other more complex systems we have quoted the results as there is insufficient space to derive them in a short book such as this.

There is an extensive bibliography on this subject and some selected references are given at the end of this chapter.

The idea of guiding electromagnetic waves by means of metallic conductors is as old as the science of electricity. It is well known that the energy guided by such means flows in the space between and around the conductors. The major difference between low frequency and high frequency guiding systems is that in the former case the spacing between the guiding conductors is extremely small compared with the wavelength, whilst in the latter the spacing is often comparable with the wavelength. The losses in a guided wave system increase with the operating frequency and very high frequency waveguides are usually restricted in length to a few hundred feet for this reason. Table 1.1 gives attenuation losses at various frequencies and illustrates this point.

Table 1.1

FREQUENCY GHz	SYSTEM	APPROXIMATE LOSS IN db/MILE
10	Co-axial cable $\frac{1}{2}$ in. o.d.	15
1,000	,, ,, ,, ,,	150
10,000	,, ,, ,, ,,	1,000
10,000	TE_{01} rectangular waveguide	250
100,000	TE_{01} ,, ,,	7,000

It is apparent that losses virtually preclude long-distance transmission at microwaves using waveguides and consequently free space transmission is normally used. The only exception to this large loss is the circular TE_{01} waveguide which has the rather peculiar property that its attenuation *decreases* as the frequency increases, the reverse of the normal trend. There are a number of technical difficulties involved in this system but many of these have been overcome. However, at the time of writing, economic reasons make the free space transmission system preferable to this particular type of waveguide transmission for the information bandwidth at present required, although this trend may change in the future.

Co-axial cables have been widely used for many years for lower frequencies, but when microwave systems were first used the cables then available were too lossy even for short lengths, and almost all microwave systems used closed rectangular pipes (waveguides) for transmission purposes. Whilst the waveguide is still used where very low loss is essential, as in either high power or low noise systems, the improvements in co-axial cables and the development of stripline have greatly altered the design of microwave systems and their components. The closed rectangular pipe is rather cumbersome mechanically and it is difficult to fabricate components using this medium. Many components can be more easily made in stripline, whilst the flexibility and ease of coupling of co-axial cables has resulted in their extensive use.

Parallel plate stripline

We will consider in some detail the parallel plate stripline as this is a simple form of waveguide which can be used to illustrate the two main types of mode that can propagate in guided wave systems. We will start by considering Maxwell's equations for free space.

$$\text{curl } \mathbf{H} = \dot{\mathbf{D}} \tag{1.1}$$

$$\text{curl } \mathbf{E} = -\dot{\mathbf{B}} \tag{1.2}$$

$$\text{div } \mathbf{D} = 0 \tag{1.3}$$

$$\text{div } \mathbf{B} = 0 \tag{1.4}$$

$$\text{where } \mathbf{B} = \mu\mathbf{H} \tag{1.5}$$

$$\mathbf{D} = \varepsilon\mathbf{E} \tag{1.6}$$

From these are obtained the wave equations

$$\nabla^2\mathbf{E} = \mu\varepsilon\ddot{\mathbf{E}} \tag{1.7}$$

$$\nabla^2\mathbf{H} = \mu\varepsilon\ddot{\mathbf{H}} \tag{1.8}$$

In the case of a simple wave in free space $\mathbf{E}$ and $\mathbf{H}$ are considered to be independent in two directions, say x and y, so (1.7) becomes

$$\frac{\partial^2\mathbf{E}}{\partial z^2} = \mu\varepsilon\frac{\partial^2\mathbf{E}}{\partial t^2} \tag{1.9}$$

This is the familiar expression for the wave on a lossless transmission system and has a solution in the form of two waves, one travelling forwards and the other backwards

$$\mathbf{E} = f_1\left(t - \frac{z}{v}\right) + f_2\left(t + \frac{z}{v}\right) \tag{1.10}$$

where

$$v = \frac{1}{\sqrt{(\mu\varepsilon)}} \tag{1.11}$$

For most practical purposes we are dealing with sinusoidal time variations only and may write

$$F(t) = e^{j\omega t} \tag{1.12}$$

so that (1.9) becomes

$$\frac{\partial^2 E}{\partial z^2} = -\omega^2 \mu \varepsilon \qquad (1.13)$$

Suppose we examine E_y only ($E_x = 0$) and consider the forward wave alone. The superscript $\pm$ denotes forward $(+)$ or backward $(-)$ waves. Then

$$E_y{}^+ = E_0 e^{+j(\omega t - \beta z)} \qquad (1.14)$$

where
$$\beta = \omega\sqrt{(\mu\varepsilon)} \qquad (1.15)$$

Remembering that the phase velocity is given by ω/β this is seen to agree with (1.11).

From (1.3), (1.6), as E and H are independent of x and y and as $E_x = 0$, it is seen that

$$\mathbf{E}_z = 0 \qquad (1.16)$$

$$\mathbf{H}_y = 0 \qquad (1.17)$$

Similarly from (1.4) and (1.5)

$$\mathbf{H}_z = 0 \qquad (1.18)$$

Thus the wave consists of E_y and H_x components only, travelling with a phase velocity given by (1.11). The relationship between these two components can be seen by examining (1.2). As

$$\frac{\partial E_y}{\partial z} = \mu \frac{\partial H_x}{\partial t}$$

it follows that

$$\frac{\partial H_x}{\partial t} = \frac{1}{\mu} \frac{\partial E_y}{\partial z} = \frac{1}{\mu} \omega\sqrt{(\mu\varepsilon)}E_0 e^{j(\omega t - \beta z)} \qquad (1.19)$$

Integrating and ignoring the constants this gives, for the forward wave only

$$H_x{}^+ = -\sqrt{\left(\frac{\varepsilon}{\mu}\right)}E_0 e^{j(\omega t - \beta z)} = -\sqrt{\left(\frac{\varepsilon}{\mu}\right)}E_y{}^+ \qquad (1.20)$$

and so

$$\frac{E_y{}^+}{H_x{}^+} = -\sqrt{\left(\frac{\varepsilon}{\mu}\right)^{-1}} = -\eta = -120\pi \text{ (or } 377\Omega) \qquad (1.21)$$

This is the wave, characteristic, or intrinsic impedance of free space. If we had assumed that field $\mathbf{E}_x$ and consequently $\mathbf{H}_y$ existed then we have found that

$$H_y{}^+ = \sqrt{\left(\frac{\varepsilon}{\mu}\right)}E_x{}^+ \qquad (1.22)$$

$$\frac{E_x^+}{H_y^+} = + \sqrt{\left(\frac{\mu}{\varepsilon}\right)} = +120\pi \text{ or } 377\Omega \qquad (1.23)$$

and if we had considered the backward wave

$$\frac{E_x^-}{H_y^-} = -\frac{E_y^-}{H_x} = -\sqrt{\left(\frac{\mu}{\varepsilon}\right)} \qquad (1.24)$$

In the simple plane wave case considered the power is propagated in z direction and the power flux density in the forward wave is given by

$$P = E \times H_{group} \qquad (1.25)$$

It is seen from (1.11) that the ~~phase~~ velocity of the wave is independent of the frequency. Remembering that the group velocity is given by $\partial\omega/\partial\beta$ it follows from (1.15) that the group velocity is given by

$$v_g = \frac{1}{\sqrt{(\mu\varepsilon)}} \qquad (1.26)$$

and is equal to the phase velocity and independent of the frequency for this TEM mode. This shows that free space is a non-dispersive transmission medium.

We will now consider a wave where only E_y exists (a vertically polarized wave) and examine the effect of introducing some perfectly

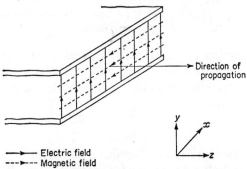

Electric field
Magnetic field

Figure 1.1. Stripline consisting of infinitely wide parallel plates. The arrow indicates the direction of propagation.

conducting metal plates that will guide the wave. At the surface of a perfect conductor only normal components of electric, and tangential components of magnetic fields can exist. Thus if a pair of parallel plates are placed so that their surfaces are horizontal only E_y and H_x components of field can be present at the surface of the plates. It is seen from Fig. 1.1 that a pair of plates could be inserted in a space carrying a vertically polarized plane wave without disturbing the fields, if the plates are infinitely wide. It is also apparent that the power density in the wave must remain constant as it is not possible for the wave to diverge at all.

The wave travelling between the plates will obey the equations just derived for free space waves and the characteristic impedance of the line formed by the plates will be determined by their spacing and width as well as the characteristic impedance of free space. If the spacing between the plates is a metres then impedance per unit width of the line is $377a\,\Omega$.

So far we have not considered the loss in the lines. These will result in a complex propagation constant and characteristic impedance and power flow in a direction normal to that of propagation. The propagation constant is then written as

$$\gamma = \alpha + j\beta \tag{1.27}$$

In practical cases the losses are such that the field pattern can be taken as the same as in the lossless case. The finite attenuation, however, is of the greatest importance. The skin depth at high frequencies is usually small compared with the conductor thickness and it is possible to work in terms of the surface resistivity of the plates R_s given by

$$R_s = \sqrt{\left(\frac{\pi f \mu}{\sigma}\right)} \quad \begin{array}{l} \mu = \text{permeability of conductor} \\ \sigma = \text{conductivity} \end{array} \tag{1.28}$$

A consideration of the boundary conditions enables the power loss to be found and this, when compared with the power flow, gives the attenuation. For an ideal parallel plate line the attenuation constant α is given by

$$\alpha = \frac{R_s}{\sqrt{(\mu/\varepsilon)a}} = \frac{R_s}{Z_0} \tag{1.29}$$

where Z_0 is the characteristic impedance of the line.

If a lossy dielectric is used then further losses occur. If the effective conductivity of the dielectric is G mho/m³ then the attenuation is given by

$$\alpha \simeq \frac{\sqrt{(\mu/\varepsilon)}.G}{2} + \frac{R_s}{Z_0} \tag{1.30}$$

These expressions only hold for the ideal line of infinite width.

The power-handling capacity of parallel plate lines is determined by the breakdown strength of the dielectric used. If this is air at normal atmospheric pressure then the breakdown strength for an infinitely wide parallel plate line is 1,200 kW/cm².

Practical form of stripline

The simplest form of stripline is a pair of parallel plates of finite width. The change from the infinitely wide plates considered in the previous section to this configuration results in a distortion of the field patterns with some field fringing into the space outside the line. Thus there may be some transverse radiation from this line and the wave propagating between the plates is no longer a pure TEM wave. However, if the spacing between the plates is made very small compared with the wavelength, then the radiation is small and a low loss transmission system results. This type of line is balanced but for many purposes an unbalanced system is preferable and the triplate line of Fig. 1.2(*a*) is used. Here the centre conductor is sandwiched between two conducting ground plates. Fig. 1.2(*b*) shows the

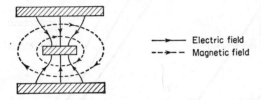

Electric field
Magnetic field

Figure 1.2(a). Triplate line.

range of impedances obtained with this line. This type of line is very convenient for the construction of a number of microwave components as the centre conductor may have various branches between the two ground plates to form microwave circuits. A simple example is the three-port stripline circulator (Chapter 7).

A more versatile form of stripline, which lends itself to the construction of integrated circuits, is the microstrip. Basically, this is a 'single wire and ground' type of line but the single strip is spaced from the ground plane by a dielectric sheet and a cover is sometimes provided to prevent radiation, as shown in Fig. 1.2(*c*). Quite complex microwave circuits may be made by the printed circuit technique. A teflon impregnated fibreglass or polystyrene board has a thin copper or silver film deposited on one side whilst on the other side the stripline printed circuit is printed by the usual means. The striplines are about $\frac{1}{16}$ to $\frac{1}{8}$ in thick. In addition to the stripline connections, many stripline components, couplers, filters, hybrid rings, etc. may be printed on the board.

A further extension of this technique is to use low conductivity silicon or gallium arsenide as the insulating material. Experiments have shown that such a stripline has a loss that very closely approaches the loss inherent in the conductors themselves. Obviously

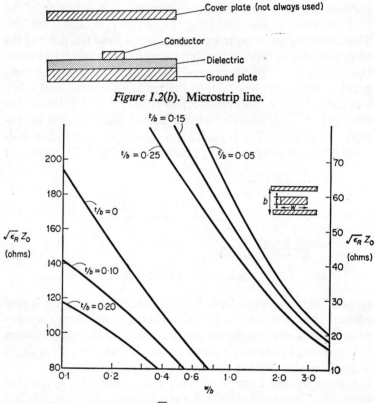

Figure 1.2(b). Microstrip line.

Figure 1.2(c). Variation of $\sqrt{\varepsilon_r}z_0$ versus W/b for triplate with various values of t/b.

(Reproduced from the *Microwave Engineers' Handbook*, 1965, p. 81, by permission of the Microwave Journal.)

the use of semiconductors as the dielectric opens up the possibility of entirely integrated microwave circuits.

It is also possible to produce microstrip circuits using thin film techniques, the dielectric being a film of SiO_2. However, in order to obtain a reasonable line impedance with the very small line spacing that results from this method of construction, a very narrow line has to be made.

Whereas the calculations necessary to find the field pattern and propagation characteristics of totally enclosed transmission systems, such as the co-axial cable or the hollow waveguide, are fairly straightforward and result in analytical expressions for the propagation constant in terms of the line dimensions and dielectric constant, similar calculations for striplines present some difficulty. The boundary problem for structures such as the microstrip line is by no means a simple one and in all types of stripline a considerable amount of energy must propagate in the fringing field. Some early attempts were made to obtain approximate analytical expressions for the stripline properties but these were found to disagree with measured results. The most successful approach seems to be that of Wheeler [1]. His approach was to use conformal mapping to find the field in the stripline in the absence of a dielectric and, where a dielectric strip is present, to allow for the distorting influence of the dielectric strip. The results may be used to compute charts which give the required parameters in terms of the ratio of strip spacing to width and various other dimensional ratios. These charts are available for all the line configurations generally used.

Although the field pattern in a stripline is not a true TEM pattern, it has a propagation constant that does not greatly differ from that of a wave in a truly TEM system with a similar dielectric constant. The problem of coupling stripline to other transmission systems is dealt with in Chapter 9.

Stripline is becoming increasingly widely used as a medium in which to construct both single microwave components and for constructing complete microwave circuits. It is not used to connect together separate components, partly due to its loss and partly due to the difficulty of making a simple and satisfactory plug and socket arrangement in stripline. Stripline components, or assemblies, are usually provided with co-axial connecting sockets.

At present the trend in the microwave field is to produce integrated circuits. For this application only stripline can be used and this medium will play an increasingly important part in the future microwave systems.

We have already mentioned that the spacing between the strips in the parallel plate line is limited by considerations of power radiation. However there is another limitation if we wish to restrict the possible mode of operation to the TEM wave. In the simple picture of the line it was shown that a plane wave would not be disturbed by the insertion of the parallel plates. This does not necessarily mean that

B

a TEM wave is the *only* one that can exist between the plates. The more rigorous consideration of the next section shows that other modes can exist if the spacing is more than $\lambda/2$ where λ is the wavelength in the dielectric material between the plates. In practice it is necessary to make the spacing much less than this in order to reduce the radiation losses to a reasonable value.

It is possible to treat the parallel plate line in a different manner by taking the expression for propagation on a lossless transmission line. The series inductance, L, and the shunt capacitance, C, could be found from purely static considerations and the propagation constant found from the expression

$$\beta = \omega\sqrt{(LC)} \qquad (1.31)$$

For the infinitely wide parallel plates the L and C values are given by

$$L = \mu(a/b) \qquad (1.32)$$

$$C = \varepsilon(b/a) \qquad (1.33)$$

Hence the propagation constant becomes

$$\beta = \omega\sqrt{(\mu\varepsilon)} \qquad (1.34)$$

which is the same as that obtained for the wave in free space. The disadvantage of this approach to the problem is that it is difficult to see, physically, why the product LC always adjusts itself to give the same value and hence the same phase velocity regardless of the shape of the line! By treating the line as a means of guiding the TEM wave it is apparent that the medium between the lines, and not the plates themselves, controls the velocity of propagation.

Other modes in parallel plate lines

So far we have shown that a TEM wave can exist between a pair of parallel plates providing that the electric field is normal to the surface of the plates. In this case there were no components of electric field parallel to, nor of magnetic field normal to, the conducting plates at any point within the guide. Another possible solution of the boundary condition is that parallel electric and normal magnetic fields should exist but have such a distribution that they drop to zero at the surface of the conducting plates. The solution of Maxwell's equations for a plane wave do not allow such a condition so we must examine the wave equations to see if other types of waves can exist. It is found that other forms of waves can exist between the plates but only if transverse components of E and H are present.

We assume that the other classes of waves propagate in a manner given by exp (j$\omega t - \gamma z$). Then in rectangular coordinates the curl equations (1.1) and (1.2) in full become for (1.1)

$$\frac{\partial E_z}{\partial y} + \gamma E_y = -j\omega\mu H_x \tag{1.32}$$

$$-\gamma E_x - \frac{\partial E_z}{\partial x} = -j\omega\mu H_y \tag{1.33}$$

$$\frac{\partial E_y}{\partial x} - \frac{\partial E_x}{\partial y} = -j\omega\mu H_z \tag{1.34}$$

and for (1.2)

$$\frac{\partial H_z}{\partial y} + \gamma H_y = j\omega\varepsilon E_x \tag{1.35}$$

$$-\gamma H_x - \frac{\partial H_z}{\partial x} = j\omega\varepsilon E_y \tag{1.36}$$

$$\frac{\partial H_y}{\partial x} - \frac{\partial H_x}{\partial y} = j\omega\varepsilon E_z \tag{1.37}$$

These equations can be rewritten to express E_x, E_y, H_x and H_y in terms of E_z and H_z

$$H_x = \frac{1}{\gamma^2 + k^2}\left[j\omega\varepsilon\frac{\partial E_z}{\partial y} - \gamma\frac{\partial H_z}{\partial x}\right] \tag{1.38}$$

$$H_y = -\frac{1}{\gamma^2 + k^2}\left[j\omega\varepsilon\frac{\partial E_z}{\partial x} + \gamma\frac{\partial H_z}{\partial y}\right] \tag{1.39}$$

$$E_x = -\frac{1}{\gamma^2 + k^2}\left[\gamma\frac{\partial E_z}{\partial x} + j\omega\mu\frac{\partial H_z}{\partial y}\right] \tag{1.40}$$

$$E_y = \frac{1}{\gamma^2 + k^2}\left[-\gamma\frac{\partial E_z}{\partial y} + j\omega\mu\frac{\gamma H_z}{\partial x}\right] \tag{1.41}$$

where $k^2 = \omega^2\mu\varepsilon$.

This form of the curl equation illustrates an important feature of the waves. If the factor $1/(\gamma^2 + k^2)$ has a finite value then H_z and/or E_z must have finite values if the x and y components of field (and hence the wave itself) is to exist. The only case where $1/(\gamma^2 + k^2)$ is not finite is where $\gamma = jk$ in which case the factor is infinite. This case is the one just considered of the plane wave. Thus there are two general forms of wave that can exist. Plane waves, whose velocity is independent of frequency and always given by $1/\sqrt{(\mu\varepsilon)}$. These waves have only transverse components of E or H. The other class of waves has a more complex form of propagation constant and has components of E and/or H in the direction of propagation. These waves have velocities that are not independent of frequency.

The wave equations for the second class of waves where $\gamma \neq k$ may be written as

$$\nabla_{xy}^2 \mathbf{E} = -(\gamma^2 + k^2)\mathbf{E} \tag{1.42}$$

$$\nabla_{xy}^2 \mathbf{H} = -(\gamma^2 + k^2)\mathbf{H} \tag{1.43}$$

It is convenient to consider separately the waves that have transverse components of magnetic field, but not of electric, and those that have transverse electric, but not magnetic, field.

Transverse magnetic waves between infinitely wide parallel conducting plates

We assume that there is a transverse electric field $\mathbf{E}_y$ that has a constant amplitude in space, and that a longitudinal field $\mathbf{E}_z$ exists. Consider now equation (1.42). The right-hand side of this equation may be expanded thus:

$$\triangle_{xy}^2 \mathbf{E} = i\left(\frac{\partial^2}{\partial x^2}\mathbf{E}_x + \frac{\partial^2}{\partial y^2}\mathbf{E}_x\right) + \mathrm{j}\left(\frac{\partial^2}{\partial x^2}\mathbf{E}_v + \frac{\partial^2}{\partial y^2}\mathbf{E}_v\right)$$
$$+ k\left(\frac{\partial^2}{\partial x^2}\mathbf{E}_z + \frac{\partial^2}{\partial y^2}\mathbf{E}_z\right)$$

The terms containing $\partial/\partial x^2$ are zero as the line is infinitely wide in the x direction. Also $\mathbf{E}_x$ is zero and $\mathbf{E}_y$ is constant so that $\partial^2/\partial y^2$ is zero and hence there is only one finite term in the expansion. Hence for the particular case under consideration (1.42) becomes

$$\frac{\partial^2 \mathbf{E}_z}{\partial y^2} = -K^2 \mathbf{E}_z \tag{1.44}$$

where $$K^2 = \gamma^2 + k^2 = \gamma^2 + \omega^2 \mu\varepsilon \tag{1.45}$$

writing the solution to (1.44) in terms of sinusoid gives

$$\mathbf{E}_z = A \sin Ky \tag{1.46}$$

As $\mathbf{E}_z$ is parallel to the surface of the conductors it must be zero at the surface and for this condition to be satisfied there must be an integral number of half periods between the two plates, i.e.

$$Ka = n\pi \tag{1.47}$$

Then remembering that $\mathbf{H}_z = 0$ and $\partial/\partial x = 0$ the other field components may be found using (1.32) to (1.37). This gives that

$$E_z = A \sin\left(\frac{n\pi y}{a}\right) \tag{1.48}$$

$$E_y = -\frac{\gamma}{K^2}\cdot\frac{\partial E_z}{\partial y} = -\frac{\gamma}{K}\cdot A \cos\left(\frac{n\pi y}{a}\right) \tag{1.49}$$

$$H_x = -\frac{j\omega\varepsilon}{K^2}\frac{\partial E_z}{\partial x} = -\frac{j\omega\varepsilon}{K}A \cos\left(\frac{n\pi y}{a}\right) \tag{1.50}$$

$$H_y = 0 \tag{1.51}$$

$$E_x = 0 \tag{1.52}$$

A number of important features of the transverse magnetic modes are given in the above equations. Firstly the propagation constant is given by

$$\gamma^2 = \sqrt{(K^2 - k^2)} = \sqrt{\left[\left(\frac{n\pi}{a}\right)^2 - \omega^2\mu\varepsilon\right]} \tag{1.53}$$

For a given spacing between the plates, a, it is seen that γ depends on the number of half periods between the plates and the angular frequency. The value of n is always an integer and is referred to as the mode number. For any particular mode number it is seen that the propagation constant will be real ($\gamma = \alpha$) if the frequency is low enough for the condition

$$\left(\frac{n\pi}{a}\right)^2 > \omega^2\mu\varepsilon \tag{1.54}$$

to be satisfied. In this case the wave suffers attenuation, but no phase shift along the direction of propagation and the guide is said to be 'cut-off'. The critical condition occurs when $(n\pi/a) = \omega\mu\varepsilon$, this value of ω being the cut-off frequency. For frequencies above this value the propagation constant is imaginary (i.e. $\gamma = j\beta$) so that the wave suffers phase shift, but no attenuation. This is the range of most interest and here it is seen that the phase and group velocities are given by

$$v_p = \frac{\omega}{\beta} = \frac{1}{\sqrt{(\mu\varepsilon)}}\cdot\frac{1}{\sqrt{[1 - (f_c/f)^2]}} \tag{1.55}$$

$$v_g = \frac{\partial\omega}{\partial\beta} = \frac{1}{\sqrt{(\mu\varepsilon)}}\cdot\sqrt{[1 - (f_c/f)^2]} \tag{1.56}$$

where f_c is the cut-off frequency given by $f_c = n/2a\sqrt{(\mu\varepsilon)}$ and the wavelength in the guide is given by

$$\lambda_g = \frac{\lambda}{\sqrt{[1 - (f_c/f)^2]}} = \frac{\lambda}{\sqrt{[1 - (\lambda/\lambda_c)^2]}} \tag{1.58}$$

where λ is the TEM wavelength at frequency f, λ_c is the TEM wavelength at frequency f_c.

The expression for the wave impedance of the TM wave is more complicated than that of the TEM wave. In the TEM case only E_x and H_y or H_y and E_x existed so that there was only one possible way of defining the wave impedance. In the TM wave components of H_x, E_y and E_z exist so that more than one impedance can be defined. However we are normally only interested in the impedance in the direction of the power flow so that E_y/H_x is the required impedance. From (1.49) and (1.50) the ratio is seen to be

$$Z_{yx} = \frac{E_y}{H_x} = \frac{\gamma}{j\omega\varepsilon} = \frac{\sqrt{[(n\pi/a)^2 - \omega^2\mu\varepsilon]}}{j\omega\varepsilon} \tag{1.59}$$

It is seen that Z_{yx} is independent of x or y and hence is the same over the whole cross-section of the guide. Again it is convenient to consider the condition where γ is imaginary. We may write $\gamma = j\beta$ so the wave impedance becomes

$$Z_{yx} = \frac{\beta}{\omega\varepsilon} \tag{1.60}$$

The important differences between the characteristics of the TM and the TEM modes may now be summarized:

(i) Lossless propagation only occurs above a certain frequency for a given mode.

(ii) An infinite number of possible modes can occur (but not at any frequency).

(iii) For frequencies above cut-off the phase velocity is greater, and the group velocity less, than that of the TEM wave in the same medium.

(iv) Phase and group velocities are functions of frequency.

(v) The wave impedance is a function of frequency.

In the case of an air-filled guide the phase velocity exceeds that in free space although the group velocity does not. This can be explained physically by the fact that the wave patterns defined in the equations can be produced by two TEM waves travelling at an angle to the axis of the guide. The phase velocity is then represented by the point of intersection of the two waves and this intersection travels faster than the waves themselves.

The various types of modes are designated by writing TM_{n0} where the zero denotes the absence of variations in the x direction and the 'n' the number of half periods in the y direction.

The effect of finite losses on both the conductors and any dielectric can again be evaluated. However the TM modes are not of great importance in stripline and the losses will not be considered here.

Transverse electric waves

In this case H_z exists but $E_z = 0$ and, in a similar manner to the previous case, we obtain

$$H_z = B \cos Ky \tag{1.61}$$

and the equations for the field components are

$$H_y = -\frac{\gamma}{K^2}\frac{\partial H_z}{\partial x} = \frac{\gamma}{K}.B \sin Ky \tag{1.62}$$

$$E_x = \frac{j\omega\mu}{K^2}\frac{\partial H_z}{\partial x} = -\frac{j\omega\mu}{K}.B \sin Ky \tag{1.63}$$

$$E_y = H_x = 0 \tag{1.64}$$

The cut-off frequency is again given by

$$f_c = \frac{n}{2a\sqrt{(\mu\varepsilon)}} \tag{1.65}$$

and guide wavelength, phase and group velocity above cut-off are given by, again, (1.55) and (1.56), not (1.58). The wave impedance is now E_x/H_y and is obtained from (1.62) and (1.63).

Above cut-off the impedance is thus given by

$$Z_{xy} = \frac{\omega\mu}{\beta} \tag{1.66}$$

The transverse waves in parallel plate lines have been dealt with in some detail, not because they are of great practical importance, but because they illustrate in a simple manner the properties of the TM and TEM waves. The analysis also shows that if the propagation is to be restricted to TEM waves then the spacing between the plates must be less than $\lambda/2$. However, restrictions due to radiation fields are rather more stringent and generally necessitate the spacing being less than this amount anyhow.

In the equation for γ (1.53) it is possible to make n zero. It is seen that the longitudinal variations of field then disappear and the propagation constant becomes $\gamma = jk$. This is simply the condition for the TEM wave to exist on the line and thus the condition that we postulated in the previous section has been proved also by the general equations.

The co-axial cable

If the parallel plate system, supporting the TEM mode, that has been previously considered, is left straight in the z direction but is bent round a curve of very large radius so that the two edges join together, then a co-axial cable of large diameter is formed. If the diameter of the curve is large enough then the fields between the plates would be virtually undisturbed. It is also apparent that if the original parallel plate system were supporting a TE or TM this also could continue

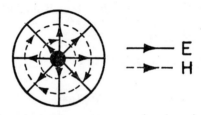

Figure 1.3(a). Field configuration in co-axial cable.

to exist in the co-axial system. An advantage of this system over the stripline is that there are now no radiating edges.

In practice the radii or curvatures are never so large that the field pattern is the same as in the parallel plate system and for the TEM system the pattern is as shown in Fig. 1.3(a). As with all TEM systems the velocity of propagation is given by $1/\sqrt{(\mu\varepsilon)}$ and is independent of the frequency.

A consideration of the boundary conditions gives the characteristic impedance as

$$Z_0 = \frac{1}{2\pi} \log_e \left(\frac{r_o}{r_i}\right).377 \text{ ohms} \qquad (1.67)$$

where r_o = diameter of outer, r_i = diameter of inner.

The dependence of Z_0 on the logarithm of the ratio of the radii makes it difficult to obtain a large range of characteristic impedances, and values less than 20 Ω or more than 150 Ω are seldom found.

Co-axial cable systems normally use the TEM mode and, in a manner similar to that of the parallel plate line, this is the only mode that can exist, provided that the spacing between the inner and outer is less than half a wavelength in the medium with which the cable is filled. Thus for very high frequencies the diameter of the cable has to be quite small.

Practical forms of co-axial cable

The inner conductor of the co-axial cable may be of solid copper or stranded copper, depending on the degree of flexibility required. The

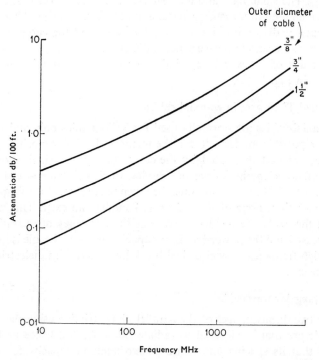

Figure 1.3(b). Variation of attenuation with frequency for various sizes of co-axial cables.

outer conductor is usually a braiding made of fine copper wires. This type of outer conductor is not as satisfactory as a solid metal outer as it allows a certain amount of r.f. radiation to occur, and movement or flexing of the cable causes changes in the attenuation and electrical noise. Solid outer conductors are seldom used but a plated outer of a corrugated form, rather similar to the flexible metal tubing used in vacuum systems, can give a performance almost equal to that of a solid outer. The conducting coating is plated directly on the corrugated dielectric of the cable.

The dielectric filling the space between the inner and outer conductors is generally a low-loss plastic. Solid or foam material or in some cases a helical strip of material, is used so that the volume of dielectric used per unit length of cable is reduced to a minimum.

Co-axial cable is now widely adopted for connecting microwave components together and can be used at low and medium power levels. The small loss, and uniformity, of modern cables is such that it can be used in measuring systems up to about 5 GHz. Above this frequency discontinuities in both the cable and the cable connectors make accurate measurements difficult to make.

Details of a few cables suitable for microwave applications are given in Fig. 1.3(b).

TE and TM waves in co-axial cables

Co-axial cables are normally used for TEM modes only and so the other possible modes will only be mentioned briefly here. The properties are best illustrated by the curves of Fig. 1.4 which show the cut-off wavelengths for various modes. In choosing a co-axial cable to carry a TEM mode care must be taken to see that, at the frequency of operation, none of the TE or TM modes can exist. This means that the cable size has to decrease as the frequency of operation is increased and the power-handling capacity of co-axial cable is limited at high frequencies by electrical breakdown as well as dielectric loss problems.

Rectangular waveguides

The two disadvantages of the parallel plate stripline using the TEM mode are that it will tend to radiate sideways, and hence be lossy, and that its spacing and hence power-handling capacity for strips of reasonable width are rather limited. Both these disadvantages can be overcome by closing in the sides of the line with further metal.

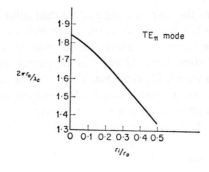

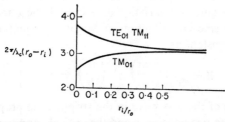

Figure 1.4. Cut-off wavelengths for various TE and TM modes in co-axial cables (r_o and r_i are the radii of the outer and inner conductor).

The guide, so formed, obviously cannot support a TEM mode as the additional boundary conditions imposed by the side walls preclude the simple field pattern of the stripline.

The field solutions for the rectangular waveguide are found in a manner similar to those for the TE or TM waves in the parallel

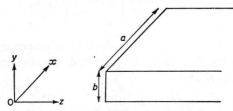

Figure 1.5. Coordinate system for waveguides.

plate line. However there are now two sets of boundary conditions to consider and if we use the symbol a to denote one dimension of the guide and b to denote the other, then using the notation of Fig. 1.5 we have

$$\left.\begin{aligned} \mathrm{E}_x = \mathrm{E}_z = 0 \text{ at } y = 0 \text{ and } y = b \\ \mathrm{E}_y = \mathrm{E}_z = 0 \text{ at } x = 0 \text{ and } x = a \end{aligned}\right\} (1.68)$$

As in the case of the stripline, the electric field must either be zero or follow a sine law with zeros at the guide walls. Once again it is found that below a certain frequency the propagation constant is real and the guide attenuates. Above this frequency the constant is imaginary and a wave will propagate. The following equations apply to the frequency range over which lossless propagation occurs and assume that the attenuation constant, α, is zero.

Again it is best to consider the TE and TM modes separately.

Transverse magnetic waves

Here a component of E_z exists and in order that E_z may be zero at the walls of the guide the variation of E_z in both the x and y direction must follow a sine law. Solution of Maxwell's equations gives the propagation constant as

$$\gamma = \sqrt{\left[\left(\frac{m\pi}{a}\right)^2 + \left(\frac{n\pi}{b}\right)^2 - \omega^2\mu\varepsilon\right]} \qquad (1.69)$$

As in the case of the TM wave in the stripline the propagation will be lossless when γ is imaginary and the critical condition is given by

$$\omega\sqrt{(\mu\varepsilon)} = \sqrt{\left[\left(\frac{m\pi}{a}\right)^2 + \left(\frac{n\pi}{b}\right)^2\right]}$$

or

$$f_c = \frac{1}{2\pi\sqrt{(\mu\varepsilon)}}\sqrt{\left[\left(\frac{m\pi}{a}\right)^2 + \left(\frac{n\pi}{b}\right)^2\right]} \qquad (1.70)$$

When γ is imaginary we may write it as $j\beta$ and hence

$$\beta = \sqrt{\left[\omega^2\mu\varepsilon - \left(\frac{m\pi}{a}\right)^2 - \left(\frac{n\pi}{b}\right)^2\right]} \qquad (1.71)$$

Thus there are a doubly infinite set of modes for lossless propagation. The cut-off frequency f_c defined by (1.69) and the corresponding cut-off wavelength is given by

$$\lambda_c = \frac{2}{\sqrt{\left[\left(\frac{m}{a}\right)^2 + \left(\frac{n}{b}\right)^2\right]}} \qquad (1.72)$$

and the phase velocity by

$$v_p = \frac{\omega}{\beta} = \frac{\omega}{\sqrt{\left[\omega^2\mu\varepsilon - \left(\frac{m\pi}{a}\right)^2 - \left(\frac{n\pi}{b}\right)^2\right]}} \qquad (1.73)$$

which is again greater than that for a TEM wave in the same medium. The wavelength is given by

$$\lambda_g = \frac{2\pi}{\sqrt{\left[\omega^2\mu\varepsilon - \left(\frac{m\pi}{a}\right)^2 - \left(\frac{n\pi}{b}\right)^2\right]}} \qquad (1.74)$$

which may be rewritten as

$$\lambda_g = \frac{\lambda}{\sqrt{[1 - (f_c/f)^2]}} = \frac{\lambda}{\sqrt{[1 - (\lambda/\lambda_c)^2]}} \qquad (1.75)$$

which is identical to (1.58) (for the stripline).

The various field components are found to be

$$E_z = C \sin\left(\frac{m\pi x}{a}\right) \sin\left(\frac{n\pi y}{b}\right) \qquad (1.76)$$

$$H_x = \frac{j\omega\varepsilon C}{K^2} \frac{n\pi}{b} \sin\left(\frac{m\pi x}{a}\right) \cos\left(\frac{n\pi y}{b}\right) \qquad (1.77)$$

$$H_y = \frac{-j\omega\varepsilon C}{K^2} \frac{m\pi}{a} \cos\left(\frac{m\pi x}{a}\right) \sin\left(\frac{n\pi y}{b}\right) \qquad (1.78)$$

$$E_x = \frac{-\gamma C}{K^2} \frac{m\pi}{a} \cos\left(\frac{m\pi x}{a}\right) \sin\left(\frac{n\pi y}{b}\right) \qquad (1.79)$$

$$E_y = \frac{-\gamma C}{K^2} \frac{n\pi}{b} \sin\left(\frac{m\pi x}{a}\right) \cos\left(\frac{n\pi y}{b}\right) \qquad (1.80)$$

All these equations should be compared with those for the TM wave in the stripline.

(C is a constant found by considering the launching of the wave $K^2 = \gamma^2 + \omega^2\mu\varepsilon$ as before.)

Transverse electric waves

Here E_z is zero but H_z is finite. The expressions for f_c, v_p and λ_g are found to be identical with those for the TM modes. The field components are given by

$$H_z = C \cos\left(\frac{m\pi x}{a}\right) \cos\left(\frac{n\pi y}{b}\right) \qquad (1.81)$$

$$E_x = \frac{j\omega\mu C}{K^2} \frac{n\pi}{b} \cos\left(\frac{m\pi x}{a}\right) \sin\left(\frac{n\pi y}{b}\right) \qquad (1.82)$$

$$E_y = \frac{-j\omega\mu C}{K^2} \frac{m\pi}{a} \sin\left(\frac{m\pi x}{a}\right) \cos\left(\frac{n\pi y}{b}\right) \qquad (1.83)$$

$$H_x = \frac{\gamma C}{K^2} \frac{m\pi}{a} \sin\left(\frac{m\pi x}{a}\right) \cos\left(\frac{n\pi y}{b}\right) \qquad (1.84)$$

$$H_y = \frac{\gamma C}{K^2} \frac{n\pi}{a} \cos\left(\frac{m\pi x}{a}\right) \sin\left(\frac{n\pi y}{b}\right) \qquad (1.85)$$

In this case it is seen that it is possible for waves to exist with either m or n (but not both) equal to zero.

It is seen that both the TE and the TM modes offer a doubly infinite number of possible modes. In a practical system it is highly desirable to arrange matters so that only one mode can exist at the operating frequency. Remembering that the cut-off wavelengths for both modes are given by

$$\lambda_c = \frac{2}{\sqrt{\left[\left(\frac{m}{a}\right)^2 + \left(\frac{n}{b}\right)^2\right]}} \qquad (1.86)$$

it is apparent that the dimensions a and b can be adjusted so that, at any one frequency, only one value of m and one of n can exist. By choosing to use the TE modes it is possible to make m or n zero so that only one mode can exist at certain frequencies. The TE_{10}* mode is widely used. In this mode the dimension b is made considerably smaller than $\lambda/2$ over the working range and the cut-off wavelength is then determined by the dimension a.

$$\lambda_c = 2a \qquad (1.87)$$

In the range from cut-off to that wavelength at which a second mode can exist, $\lambda_c' = 2b$, there is only one possible mode of propagation. This mode is illustrated in Fig. 1.6. A few other low-order modes are also illustrated here.

One obvious advantage of the waveguide is that the wave may be propagated in an entirely air-filled space and so that only resistive losses can cause attenuation. Analysis of the fields in a copper waveguide shows that the theoretical attenuation for the TE_{10} mode is given by

$$\alpha = \frac{87R_s}{b\eta\sqrt{[1 - (f_c/f)^2]}}\left[1 + \frac{2bf_c^2}{af^2}\right] db/m \qquad (1.88)$$

* The subscript mn is used to denote the values of m and n. In some British texts the subscript nm is used instead and the TE modes are called H modes and the TM modes E modes.

TE MODES IN RECTANGULAR WAVEGUIDE

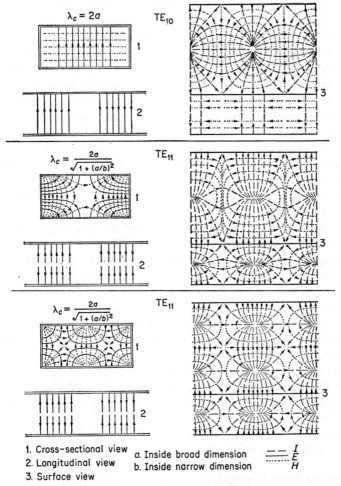

1. Cross-sectional view
2. Longitudinal view
3. Surface view

a. Inside broad dimension
b. Inside narrow dimension

$$— — \frac{I}{E}$$
$$\cdots\cdots\; H$$

Figure 1.6. Field patterns for various modes in rectangular waveguide.

For any given guide the attenuation is very large near cut-off and drops to a minimum at about twice the cut-off frequency. It then rises steadily as the frequency increases. However, in order to ensure that only the dominant mode exists it is necessary to make the dimensions of the waveguide small at high frequencies, with consequently high attenuation. A further difficulty arises in that the skin depth in the walls of the waveguide become so small at very high frequencies that the conducting walls can not longer be regarded as being smooth. This fact makes the attenuation of guides for millimetre waves much greater than that predicted theoretically.

The power-handling capacity of waveguides is simply determined by the peak value of electric field and the pressure of the air in the guide. Once again the reduction in guide size necessary at the higher frequencies restricts the power-handling capacity but even so lag powers can be handled. In cases where CW powers are being carried, operation near the breakdown point may result in a considerable rise in the temperature of the waveguide walls due to the resistive losses, but the guide can always be cooled if necessary. Usually the CW powers available from most tubes are not sufficient to make this effect troublesome. In the case of pulse systems the heating effect is generally negligible but breakdown due to the high field strength can easily occur.

If the dimensions of the waveguide, and the operating frequency, are such that several modes can exist then the mode or modes that propagate depend on the launching mechanism. It is possible to make the launching device so that only one mode is excited. Unfortunately any small variation in the size of the waveguide or any other discontinuity will cause other modes to be excited as well. As the device that receives the signal at the other end of the guide is usually only sensitive to one mode some of the power will not be received. Furthermore, the different propagation constants of the various modes will cause distortion in the information content of the signal. For these reasons almost all waveguide systems are designed so that only one mode can exist within the range of operating frequencies required.

The rectangular guide carrying the TE_{10} mode is used more than any other hollow waveguide.

Practical form of waveguide

The rectangular metal pipe is capable of supporting an infinity of TE or TM modes. The variation of attenuation with frequency for a few lower order modes is shown in Fig. 1.7. It will be seen that there is a range of frequencies just above the cut-off frequency for which only one possible mode can exist. This is known as the dominant mode and it is highly desirable to use this mode in waveguide systems. If it is possible for more than one mode to exist at any given frequency then, even though the launching mechanism is designed to launch one mode, any discontinuities, or even small imperfections in the guide, will tend to excite other modes. As the various modes have different field patterns they will only excite an output device designed for the particular mode in question and any mode conversion can result in loss of power and many undesirable effects. For satisfactory operation the guide must only be used for frequencies in the range indicated in Fig. 1.7. Thus a number of different waveguide sizes have to be used to cover the microwave spectrum.

Waveguides are usually drawn out of copper or brass and their internal dimensions are kept to a close tolerance. For frequencies below about 1 GHz the waveguide becomes very bulky. At the other

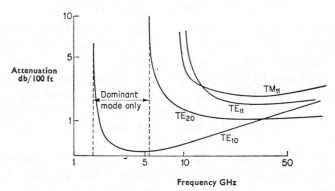

Figure 1.7. Attenuation for various modes in 1·87 in × 0·87 in rectangular waveguide.

end of the scale guides for millimetre waves are extremely small and very high tolerances are necessary to maintain a fairly uniform guide. Furthermore the extremely small skin depth at these frequencies is comparable to the surface roughness produced by normal drawing processes. This increases the loss in the guide and special techniques, such as electro-forming and metal spraying, are used to produce a better finish and so reduce the loss.

A few Standard Waveguide Sizes and their Frequency Coverage are given in Table 1.2.

Other forms of waveguide

Although only rectangular waveguides have been considered in detail it can be shown that any closed metal pipe can propagate TE or TM modes. An obvious choice of pipe is a cylindrical one as these are

C

Table 1.2. Properties and sizes of typical rectangular waveguide

INSIDE DIMENSIONS (inches)	FREQUENCY RANGE (GHz)	THEORETICAL* ATTENUATION (db/100 ft)	THEORETICAL* POWER-HANDLING CAPACITOR MW
2·30 × 11·5	0·32– 0·49	0·04	170
2·84 × 1·34	2·6 – 3·9	1·0	2·5
0·90 × 0·40	8·2 – 12·4	5·0	0·25
0·224 × 0·112	33 – 50	25	0·015
0·034 × 0·017	220 –325	400	0·00035

* Figure given is for centre of frequency range.

easy to manufacture. The field equations can be expressed in cylindrical coordinates and the resulting integers m and n then refer to the number of full periods of variation of the radial field and the number of half-periods of the angular field respectively. A few of the field patterns for lower order modes are illustrated in Fig. 1.8.

It will be seen that the dominant mode, TE_{11}, does not possess azimuthal symmetry. This means that if such a wave is launched in a circular pipe small discontinuities in the pipe will tend to make it change the plane of its field pattern so that when it is required to extract the power the correct orientation of the transducer is not known.

Other patterns do have azimuthal symmetry and the TE_{01} mode is of particular interest as it has an attenuation that decreases steadily as the frequency increases. However as it is not the dominant mode it tends to degenerate into other modes. Considerable work has been carried out on methods of suppressing these other modes and low loss TE_{01} waveguide systems have been successfully developed, usually operating at about 30 GHz. These systems offer enormous bandwidths but, at the moment, do not seem to be commercially competitive as these very wide bandwidths are seldom required. However, as the demand for communications grows, it seems likely that such systems will become economic.

A variation on the simple rectangular waveguide is the ridged guide.

Ridged waveguide

Although rectangular waveguides have the advantage of a low loss as compared with co-axial cables or striplines their frequency range

TE MODES IN CIRCULAR WAVEGUIDE

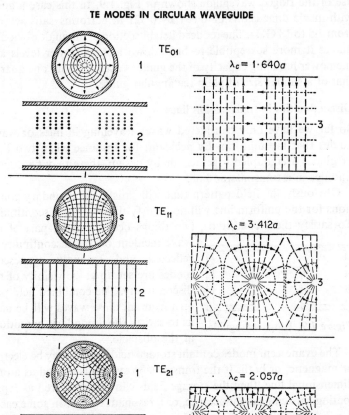

1. Cross-sectional view
2. Longitudinal view through plane /-/
3. Surface view from s—s

a. Inside broad
dimension

— — I
— — E
····· H

Figure 1.8. Field patterns in circular waveguides.

only extends from the cut-off frequency to the frequency at which higher order modes can propagate. For instance, a TE_{01} guide of inside dimensions of 0·9 by 0·4 in can only be used from 8·2 to 12·4 GHz. This rather restricted bandwidth can be improved by the use of the ridged waveguide shown in Fig. 1.9. In this case a guide with inside dimensions of 0·691 by 0·321 in performs satisfactorily from 7·5 to 18 GHz. The reduced height section of the guide obviously makes it more susceptible to breakdown at high power levels and the power handling capacity of the guide is usually about one quarter that of a similar size of plain rectangular guide.

Discontinuities in transmission lines

So far we have only considered waves travelling in lines or wave-guides that are uniform. By accident, for instance when two lines or guides are coupled together, or by design, there may be discontinuities in a transmission line.

Obviously the field pattern that will satisfy the boundary conditions for the uniform line will not satisfy those at the discontinuity. To satisfy these conditions, two things occur. Firstly, part of the wave incident on the discontinuity is reflected and secondly evanescent modes are set up in the vicinity of the discontinuity. The combined field pattern from all these waves will be such as to satisfy the boundary conditions at the obstacle.

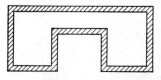

Figure 1.9. Ridge waveguide.

The evanescent modes contain storage fields which may be electric, or magnetic, or both. If the transmission system is treated as a one-dimensional line, then the storage fields can be considered as representing capacitance, inductance, or a resonant circuit. In some cases, the discontinuity can be considered as a simple shunt element, but in others the equivalent circuit may take the T or π form. However, having reduced the obstacle to its equivalent circuit, it must be remembered that, although the equivalent circuit element has no physical length, the actual fields of the evanescent modes that constitute this equivalent circuit element extend for a distance either side of the obstacle. Theoretically they extend an infinite distance either side but, due to their exponential decay, they extend only a fairly short distance for all practical purposes. Thus, if two obstacles, such as diaphragms, are placed so close together in a transmission line that their evanescent fields overlap, then the effect of the two obstacles cannot be correctly predicted from the equivalent circuit based on the equivalent reactance of each individual obstacle.

The effect of obstacles of a fairly simple geometrical form, such as diaphragms, posts, irises, has been calculated and the tabulated results are available for many configurations. Direct solution of Maxwell's equations for the particular boundary conditions under consideration is not usually possible and the variational technique is generally used.

Reference

[1] H. H. Wheeler, *Transmission Line Properties or Parallel Strips Separated by a Dielectric Sheet, I.E.E.E. Trans.*, MTT-13, 1965, 172.

Figures 1.6 and 1.8 are reproduced from Waveguide Handbook, MIT Rad. Lab. Series, vol. 10, edited by N. Marcavitz, by permission of the McGraw-Hill Book Co. Inc.

CHAPTER 2

Transmission Line Theory

Introduction

The use of waveguides, co-axial lines and striplines for the transmission of microwaves has been discussed in Chapter 1 and it has been shown that various different modes may exist in a single waveguide. Except for pure TEM waves, waveguides have a dispersive transmission characteristic; the velocity of a wave in a guide is a function of frequency as well as the type of wavemode in the guide. Although the equations describing the fields in a waveguide are more complicated than those describing the current and voltage on a two-wire transmission line carrying a TEM mode, they have the same basic form and it is useful to describe waveguide transmission in terms of a two-wire model. This model can be applied to the transmission of a continuous wave in a waveguide supporting a single mode.

A waveguide can support fields having both longitudinal and transverse components. The longitudinal components may be derived from the transverse components if the mode in the guide is known. If the transverse components of the electric and magnetic fields are E and H respectively a wave impedance may be defined as

$$Z_0 = E/H \tag{2.1}$$

This ratio of the transverse components of the fields is constant over the cross-section of the guide and may be referred to as the characteristic wave impedance by analogy with the two-wire line. The impedance Z_0 may be a function of the frequency of the wave and the waveguide mode.

The total field in the guide may be described in terms of two waves travelling in opposite directions along the guide, an incident wave and a reflected wave. The total transverse fields in the guide are given by

$$E = E^+ + E^-$$
and
$$H = H^+ + H^- \tag{2.2}$$

where the positive superscript denotes the incident wave and the negative the reflected wave. Relative to the values E_0^+, E_0^- at some reference point in the guide, the fields at a distance z towards the load are given by

$$E^+ = E_0^+e^{-\gamma z}$$
and
$$E^- = E_0^-e^{+\gamma z}$$
$\left.\vphantom{\begin{array}{c}a\\b\end{array}}\right\}(2.3)$

Here γ is a complex propagation coefficient and may be written

$$\gamma = \alpha + j\beta \qquad (2.4)$$

For a loss-free system, $\alpha = 0$ and then the wave is propagated without attenuation but with a phase change depending on the phase change coefficient β. The coefficient β will be a function of frequency in a dispersive transmission system but for a single frequency the fields are given by

$$E^+ = E_0^+e^{-j\beta z}$$
$$E^- = E_0^-e^{-j\beta z}$$
$\left.\vphantom{\begin{array}{c}a\\b\end{array}}\right\}(2.5)$

The phase change coefficient is related to the phase velocity of the wave by

$$v_p = \omega/\beta \qquad (2.6)$$

where ω is the angular frequency of the wave measured in radians/sec and the phase change coefficient is measured in radians/metre.

The total transverse fields at a point in the guide are given by

$$E = E_0^+e^{-j\beta z} + E_0^-e^{+j\beta z}$$
$$H = H_0^+e^{-j\beta z} + H_0^-e^{+j\beta z}$$
$\left.\vphantom{\begin{array}{c}a\\b\end{array}}\right\}(2.7)$

For a particular mode in the guide the directions of the field E^+ and H^+ will be polarized in orthogonal directions related by the corkscrew rule. The reflected fields are still orthogonal but in the opposite sense of rotation relative to the positive direction of propagation. As the wave impedance is independent of the direction of propagation the fields in the incident and reflected waves are given respectively by

$$H^+ = \frac{E^+}{Z_0} \qquad (2.8)$$

and
$$H^- = \frac{-E^-}{Z_0} \qquad (2.9)$$

The transverse field components may be written in terms of the electric fields at the origin as

$$E = E_0^+e^{-j\beta z} + E_0^-e^{+j\beta z} \qquad (2.10)$$

$$H = \frac{1}{Z_0}\left\{E_0^+e^{-j\beta z} - E_0^-e^{+j\beta z}\right\} \tag{2.11}$$

For H modes the wave impedance is given by

$$\frac{E^+}{H^+} = \frac{\omega\mu}{\beta} \tag{2.12}$$

and for E modes the wave impedance is given by

$$\frac{E^+}{H^+} = \frac{\beta}{\omega\varepsilon} \tag{2.13}$$

where μ and ε are the permeability and permittivity of the material filling the guide. As $\beta = \omega/v_p$ and the velocity of TEM waves in the medium is given by $v = 1/\sqrt{(\mu\varepsilon)}$, the value of Z_0 is given, for H modes by

$$Z_0 = \frac{v_p}{v}\sqrt{\left(\frac{\mu}{\varepsilon}\right)} = \frac{\lambda_g}{\lambda}\sqrt{\left(\frac{\mu}{\varepsilon}\right)} \tag{2.14}$$

and for E modes by

$$Z_0 = \frac{v}{v_p}\sqrt{\left(\frac{\mu}{\varepsilon}\right)} = \frac{\lambda}{\lambda_g}\sqrt{\left(\frac{\mu}{\varepsilon}\right)} \tag{2.15}$$

In a guide filled with loss-free dielectric, $\mu = \mu_0$ and $\varepsilon = \varepsilon_0.\varepsilon_r$.

Also
$$\frac{\lambda_g}{\lambda} = \left\{\varepsilon_r - \left(\frac{\lambda}{\lambda_c}\right)^2\right\}^{\frac{1}{2}} \tag{2.16}$$

where λ_g is the guide wavelength and λ_c is the cut-off wavelength of the guide. Substituting gives for H modes that

$$Z_0 = \frac{377}{\sqrt{\left[\varepsilon_r - \left(\frac{\lambda_0}{\lambda_c}\right)^2\right]}} \text{ ohms} \tag{2.17}$$

and for E modes that

$$Z_0 = \frac{377}{\varepsilon_r}\sqrt{\left[\varepsilon_r - \left(\frac{\lambda_0}{\lambda_c}\right)^2\right]}\text{ohms} \tag{2.18}$$

As the equations of propagation of a wave in a waveguide have the same form as those for propagation on a two-wire line and as a characteristic wave impedance can be found for a waveguide for a particular frequency, it is possible to treat single-frequency waveguide transmission problems by direct analogy with equivalent two-wire line problems. This treatment simplifies the discussion of impedance transformation and matching problems.

Reflection coefficient

If the characteristic impedance of a two-wire line is constant there is a unique relation between the E and H fields at a single frequency. In discussing the behaviour of the fields the E field will be considered primarily.

The two-wire line of characteristic impedance Z_0 is shown in Fig. 2.1 terminated by the load impedance Z at a distance z from the sending end. If the load impedance is not equal to the line

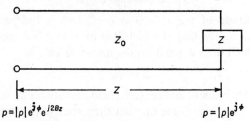

Figure 2.1. Two-wire line and reflection coefficient transformation.

impedance, part of the energy incident on the load will be reflected. Two reflection coefficients may be given in terms of the electric or magnetic fields. These are

$$\rho_E = \frac{E^-}{E^+} \tag{2.19}$$

and

$$\rho_H = \frac{H^-}{H^+} \tag{2.20}$$

In general both these reflection coefficients are complex as there is a change in both amplitude and phase between the incident and reflected waves. The two reflection coefficients are related. Substituting for H^+ and H^- from equations 2.8, 2.9 gives that

$$\rho_H = -\frac{E^-}{E^+} = -\rho_E \tag{2.21}$$

Usually the electric field reflection coefficient will be used and the symbol ρ without the subscript will denote this coefficient. As ρ is complex it may be written

$$\rho = |\rho| e^{j\phi} \tag{2.22}$$

This refers to conditions at the load. Suppose now that the fields at the source are considered and are related to those at the load i.e.

$$\left.\begin{aligned}E^+ &= E_0{}^+ e^{-j\beta z} \\ E^- &= E_0{}^- e^{+j\beta z}\end{aligned}\right\} \tag{2.23}$$

Then
$$\rho = \frac{E_0^-}{E_0^+}e^{j2\beta z} \qquad (2.24)$$

or writing
$$\frac{E_0^-}{E_0^+} = \rho_0$$

gives
$$\rho = \rho_0\,e^{j2\beta z} \qquad (2.25)$$

Writing this in terms of amplitude and phase

$$|\rho|\,e^{j\phi} = |\rho_0|\,e^{j\phi_0}.e^{j2\beta z} \qquad (2.26)$$

The amplitude of the reflection coefficient is independent of the position along the line at which it is measured but there is a phase change which does depend on the distance. This is

$$\phi = \phi_0 + 2\beta z \qquad (2.27)$$

The separate incident and reflected field amplitudes do not vary along the line but their relative phase does. This is illustrated in the circle diagram Fig. 2.2. Here the variation in fields are shown relative to the situation at the load end. The outer circle represents the amplitude of the incident wave, the inner that of the reflected wave. The two phasors show the relative phase at the load whilst the variation of phase with distance is shown by rotation of these phasors. As each rotates by an angle βz on moving the point of reference through the distance z, their relative phase and the phase of the reflection coefficient varies by $2\beta z$.

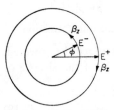

Figure 2.2. Circle diagram for reflection coefficient transformation.

The total field at a distance z from the origin is given by

$$E = E^+ + E^- \qquad (2.28)$$

Now
$$E^- = E_0^-e^{+j\beta z}$$
$$= \rho_0 E_0^+e^{+j\beta z}$$
$$= |\rho_0|\,E_0^+e^{-j\beta z}.e^{j(2\beta z + \phi_0)} \qquad (2.29)$$

Thus the total field E is given by

$$E = E^+(1 + |\rho|\,e^{j(2\beta z + \phi_0)}) \qquad (2.30)$$

Suppose now that distance is measured from the load. If E_L^+ and E_L^- refer to conditions at the load

$$E = E_L^+e^{+j\beta z} + E_L^-e^{-j\beta z} \qquad (2.31)$$

as z is measured in the reverse direction. Also at the load

$$\rho = |\rho| e^{j\phi}$$

$$= \frac{E_L{}^-}{E_L{}^+} \tag{2.32}$$

The field at z from the load can then be written as

$$E = E_L{}^+(e^{+j\beta z} + \rho e^{-j\beta z})$$

$$= E^+(1 + |\rho| e^{j(\phi_0 - 2\beta z)}) \tag{2.33}$$

Thus the total field at a distance z from the origin or the load may be

found if the reflection coefficient is known at the origin or at the load. The variation in field with distance from the load is shown in Fig. 2.3 where the phasor E^+ is taken as reference. The phasor E^- is drawn for distance z from the load. As z increases this phasor rotates

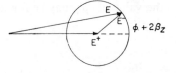

Figure 2.3. Crank diagram for field variation in standing wave.

and the resultant E varies in amplitude in a cyclic manner with distance. This variation in amplitude with distance from the load is shown in Fig. 2.4. A standing wave pattern is produced by the

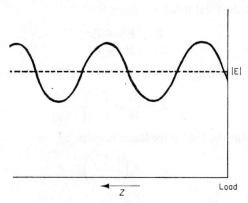

Figure 2.4. Field standing wave pattern.

interference of the incident and reflected waves. There is a minimum in this standing wave pattern when

$$\phi - 2\beta z = \pi, 3\pi, \text{etc.} \tag{2.34}$$

and a maximum when

$$\phi - 2\beta z = 0, 2\pi, \text{ etc.} \tag{2.35}$$

If the distance d_{min} or d_{max} from the load is measured, then

$$\left.\begin{aligned} \phi &= 2\beta d_{min} + (2n - 1)\pi \\ &= 2\beta d_{max} + 2n\pi \end{aligned}\right\} \tag{2.36}$$

where ϕ is the phase angle of the reflection coefficient of the load. Also, as the maximum in the field has an amplitude of $1 + |\rho|$ and the minimum has an amplitude of $1 - |\rho|$ and if the ratio of the amplitudes and the voltage standing wave ratio, v.s.w.r., is measured the value of $|\rho|$ may be found. Writing the v.s.w.r. as s,

$$s = \frac{1 - |\rho|}{1 + |\rho|} \tag{2.37}$$

or

$$|\rho| = \frac{1 - s}{1 + s} \tag{2.38}$$

Thus by measurement of the v.s.w.r. and the position of the maximum or minimum of the pattern from the load, the complex reflection coefficient of the load may be found.

Load impedance and reflection coefficient

At the load the total fields are given by

$$\left.\begin{aligned} E &= E^+ + E^- \\ H &= H^+ + H^- \end{aligned}\right\} \tag{2.39}$$

The load impedance is the ratio of the total fields at the load

$$Z = \frac{E}{H} = \frac{E^+(1 + \rho)}{H^+(1 - \rho)} \tag{2.40}$$

It follows that the load impedance is given by

$$Z = Z_0\left(\frac{1 + \rho}{1 - \rho}\right) \tag{2.41}$$

or

$$\rho = \frac{Z - Z_0}{Z + Z_0} \tag{2.42}$$

It may be convenient to write these expressions in terms of admittances to give

$$Y = Y_0\left(\frac{1 - \rho}{1 + \rho}\right) \tag{2.43}$$

and
$$\rho = \frac{Y_0 - Y}{Y_0 + Y} \qquad (2.44)$$

If the load impedance is equal to the characteristic impedance of the line, $\rho = 0$ and there is no reflection at the load. All the incident energy is absorbed in the load and the load is said to be matched to the line. Under these conditions there is no standing wave on the line.

If the load impedance is an open circuit, $Z \rightarrow \infty$ and then $\rho = 1$. There is complete reflection of the energy with the incident and reflected electric fields in phase at the open circuit. There is a doubling in the electric field at this point.

If the load is a short circuit, $Z = 0$, $\rho = -1$. There is again complete reflection of the energy but the electric fields are in antiphase so that there is zero electric field at the load.

Transformation of impedance

The effective reflection coefficient of a load impedance varies in phase according to the position on the line at which it is measured.

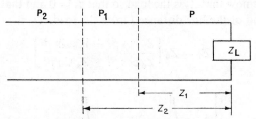

Figure 2.5. Transformation of impedance on transmission line.

In Fig. 2.5 two points are shown at distances z_1 and z_2 from the load. The reflection coefficients at these points will be

$$\rho_1 = \rho e^{-j2\beta z_1}$$
$$\rho_2 = \rho e^{-j2\beta z_2}$$

or
$$\rho_1 = \rho_2 e^{-j2\beta(z_1 - z_2)} \qquad (2.45)$$

This expression relates the reflection coefficients at two different points on the line.

The impedance presented at the point 1 is given by

$$Z_1 = Z_0\left(\frac{1 + \rho_1}{1 - \rho_1}\right) \tag{2.46}$$

and at point 2 by

$$Z_2 = Z_0\left(\frac{1 + \rho_2}{1 - \rho_2}\right) \tag{2.47}$$

The expression for Z_1 may also be written

$$Z_1 = Z_0\left[\frac{1 + \left(\dfrac{Z_2 - Z_0}{Z_2 + Z_0}\right)e^{-j2\beta(z_1 - z_2)}}{1 - \left(\dfrac{Z_2 - Z_0}{Z_2 + Z_0}\right)e^{-j2\beta(z_1 - z_2)}}\right]$$

$$= Z_0\left[\frac{(Z_2 + Z_0)e^{j\beta(z_1 - z_2)} + (Z_2 - Z_0)e^{-j\beta(z_1 - z_2)}}{(Z_2 + Z_0)e^{j(z_1 - z_2)} + (Z_2 - Z_0)e^{-j\beta(z_1 - z_2)}}\right]$$

$$= Z_0\left[\frac{Z_2 \cos \beta(z_1 - z_2) + jZ_0 \sin \beta(z_1 - z_2)}{Z_0 \cos \beta(z_1 - z_2) + jZ_2 \sin \beta(z_1 - z_2)}\right] \tag{2.48}$$

where z_1 and z_2 are distances from the load end.

Suppose now that Z_2 is the load so that $z_2 = 0$ and that z_1 is at the sending end of the line distance l from the load. Then

$$Z_1 = Z_0\left[\frac{Z_2 \cos \beta l + jZ_0 \sin \beta l}{Z_0 \cos \beta l + Z_2 \sin \beta l}\right] \tag{2.49}$$

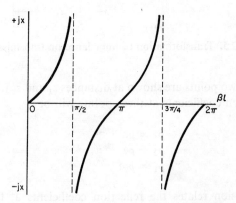

Figure 2.6. Input impedance of short circuit line.

Alternatively if Z_1 is the load so that $z_1 = 0$ and Z_2 is measured at the distance l from the load

$$Z_1 = Z_0 \left[\frac{Z_2 \cos \beta l - jZ_0 \sin \beta l}{Z_0 \cos \beta l - jZ_2 \sin \beta l} \right] \qquad (2.50)$$

If the load is a short circuit, then from equation

$$Z_1 = Z_0 \tan \beta l \qquad (2.51)$$

The sending end impedance is purely reactive and can take any positive or negative value as shown in Fig. 2.6.

Circle diagram for reflection coefficient and impedance

The transformation or reflection coefficient is given by

$$\rho_1 = \rho_2 e^{-j2\beta(z_1 - z_2)} \qquad (2.52)$$

The modulus of the reflection coefficient remains constant and is less than unity but the phase is varied by movement along the line. This is illustrated in Fig. 2.7 where the phasors for ρ_1 and ρ_2 are shown of the same length but separated by the angle $2\beta(z_1 - z_2)$, and contained within a circle of unit radius. It is useful to have some graphical method of relating the reflection coefficient to the impedance across the line. On the circle diagram for reflection coefficient it is possible to draw curves of constant normalized resistance and constant normalized reactance.

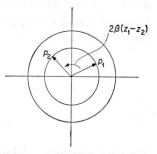

Figure 2.7. Reflection coefficient modulus and phase angle.

The normalized impedance is given by

$$\frac{Z}{Z_0} = \frac{1 + \rho}{1 - \rho}$$

Writing R and X for the normalized resistance and reactance

$$R + jX = \frac{1 + |\rho| e^{j\phi}}{1 - |\rho| e^{j\phi}} \qquad (2.53)$$

Separating real and imaginary parts

$$R = \frac{1 - |\rho|^2}{1 + |\rho|^2 + 2|\rho| \cos \phi} \qquad (2.54)$$

$$X = \frac{2\,|\,\rho\,|\,\sin\phi}{1 + |\,\rho\,|^2 - 2\,|\,\rho\,|\cos\phi} \tag{2.55}$$

From these the locus of $|\,\rho\,| < \phi$ may be found for constant values of R or X. Cross multiplying gives

$$|\,\rho\,|^2 - \frac{2R}{R+1}|\,\rho\,|\cos\phi = \frac{R-1}{R+1} \tag{2.56}$$

and

$$|\,\rho\,|^2 - 2\,|\,\rho\,|\left(\cos\phi + \frac{\sin\phi}{x}\right) = -1 \tag{2.57}$$

In rectangular coordinates the equation of a circle of radius c, centre (a, b) is

$$(x - a)^2 + (y - b)^2 = c^2 \tag{2.58}$$

Writing
$$\left.\begin{aligned} x &= |\,\rho\,|\cos\phi \\ y &= |\,\rho\,|\sin\phi \end{aligned}\right\} \tag{2.59}$$

gives $|\,\rho\,|^2 - 2\,|\,\rho\,|\,(a\cos\phi + b\sin\phi) = c^2 - (a^2 + b^2)$ (2.60)

Comparing equation (2.56) with equation (2.60) gives for lines of constant resistance

$$\left.\begin{aligned} a &= \frac{R}{R+1} \\ b &= 0 \\ c &= \frac{1}{R+1} \end{aligned}\right\} \tag{2.61}$$

and

The circles so defined all pass through the point $x = 1$, $y = 0$. The family of circles for different values of R are shown in Fig. 2.8. Comparing equations 2.57, 2.60, gives for lines of constant reactance that

$$\left.\begin{aligned} a &= 1 \\ b &= \frac{1}{X} \\ c &= \frac{1}{X} \end{aligned}\right\} \tag{2.62}$$

Again all the circles pass through $x = 1$, $y = 0$ and their centres lie on the line, $x = 1$, parallel to the y axis. The family of curves for constant x is shown in Fig. 2.9.

The combined figure for values of R and X is shown in Fig. 2.10. On this figure is plotted a reflection coefficient $|\,\rho\,| < \phi$ showing that this relates to definite values of R and X. If this phasor is rotated through the angle $2\beta z$, new values of R and X are given corresponding to the new position after movement distance z along the line.

The measurements that it is convenient to make on a line are those

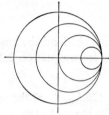

Circles of constant R

Figure 2.8. Impedance circle diagram. Lines of constant resistance, R.

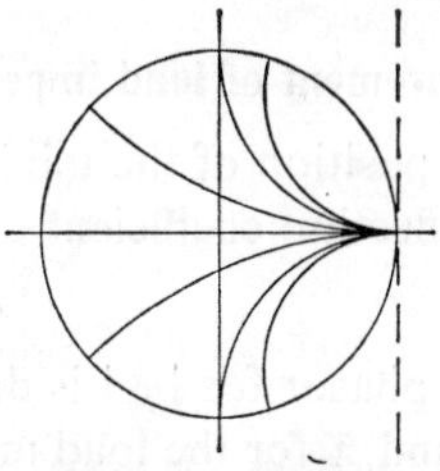

Circles of constant X

Figure 2.9. Impedance circle diagram. Lines of constant reactance, X.

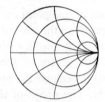

Circles of constant R and X

Figure 2.10. Impedance circle diagram with lines of constant R and X.

of v.s.w.r. and the position of a minimum in the standing wave pattern. The modulus of ρ is given by

$$|\rho| = \frac{1-s}{1+s}$$

and also

$$|\rho| = \frac{Z-Z_0}{Z+Z_0}$$

If z and z_0 are real

$$|\rho| = \frac{R-1}{R+1}$$

and then

$$s = \frac{1}{R} \qquad\qquad (2.63)$$

Thus as the line of $x = 0$ on the circle diagram is the real axis,

D

values of R on the axis correspond to values of s and circles centred at the origin drawn through values of $R = 1/s$ are circles of constant s or $|\rho|$. As the scale of R on one side of the origin is the inverse of that on the opposite side, a circle through $s = R$ on one side passes through $s = 1/R$ on the other.

Measurement of load impedance

If the position of the minimum is at d_{min} from the load the angle of the reflection coefficient of the load is given from equation 2.36 by

$$\phi = 2\beta d_{min} + \pi$$

If the phasor for $|\rho|$ is drawn at the angle $(2\beta d_{min} + \pi)$ the values of R and X for the load may be read from the chart. As the position $+\pi$ is at -1 on the real axis, the angle ϕ is given by rotation through $2\beta d_{min}$ from this position in an anti-clockwise direction.

Transformation of impedance

If the normalized impedance at one point on the transmission line is known the corresponding point on the circle diagram may be located. If the transformed impedance at another point is required it must lie on a circle centred at the centre of the diagram and passing through the first point. This is because the modulus of the reflection coefficient remains constant. The phase of the reflection coefficient changes by $2\beta z$ where z is the distance moved along the line. If the second point is further from the generator than the first, the change in phase is positive corresponding to anti-clockwise rotation on the chart. Clockwise rotation corresponds to movement towards the generator.

Use of circle diagram with transmission lines with loss

If there is absorption or loss in the transmission line the propagation constant γ is given by

$$\gamma = \alpha + j\beta$$

where α now has a real finite value. The total electric field is given by

$$E = E^+ + E^-$$
$$= E_0^+ e^{-\alpha z} e^{-j\beta z} + E_0^- e^{+\alpha z} e^{+j\beta z} \tag{2.64}$$

and as before the reflection coefficient is given by

$$\rho = \frac{E_0^-}{E_0^+} e^{2\alpha z} e^{j2\beta z}$$

$$= \rho_0 e^{2\alpha z} e^{j2\beta z}$$

$$= |\rho| e^{2\alpha z} e^{(2\beta z + \phi_0)} \qquad (2.65)$$

The modulus of the reflection coefficient now varies as $e^{2\alpha}$ and on moving towards the generator, i.e. as z decreases, $|\rho|$ decreases. On the circle diagram the locus of $|\rho|$ is then a spiral which may be plotted if α is known.

In the case of a lossy line the characteristic impedance becomes complex and the impedances measured are normalized to the complex impedance.

Circle diagram for admittance

The circle diagram may be used for admittances instead of impedances. The locus of lines of constant G and B may be found by a similar method to those for R and X. It is found that the circles of R correspond to those for G and those of X to those for B. It should be remembered that although the numerical values correspond, a positive reactance corresponds to a negative susceptance.

It is often simpler to work in admittances if components in parallel across a line are being considered.

Matching

When a transmission line is terminated by a load impedance, some of the incident power is in general reflected from the load. This is generally undesirable as not only is the amount of power absorbed by the load less than the power available from the source, but also a standing wave is set up on the transmission line. A standing wave is undesirable on the transmission line in high power systems because the increased voltages on the line may lead to breakdown. In communication systems, the presence of reflected waves on the transmission line may lead to distortion of the signal.

For there to be no reflected wave on the transmission line, the load impedance must be made equal to the characteristic impedance of the line. The load is then said to be matched to the line. The matching of load to line may be carried out by inserting additional components between the load and the line. The components may be resistive or reactive. Resistive components can have values independent of frequency but they introduce loss. Reactive components can be loss free but generally are frequency sensitive.

In microwave transmission systems, matching is usually carried out with reactive components, but the system should be designed with components which are inherently well matched over a broad-band to reduce the effect of frequency variations on the system.

The reactive components which may be used for matching are open circuit and short circuit transmission lines in series or shunt with the main transmission line or obstacles such as posts or diaphragms placed in the transmission line. The reactive properties and construction of these devices will be discussed in more detail in Chapter 4.

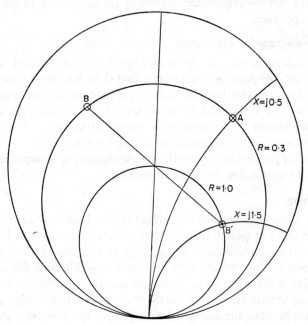

Figure 2.11. Circle diagram and impedance matching.

The devices used for matching often appear as shunt reactances across the transmission. When considering components in parallel across the transmission line, it is easier to consider their admittances rather than their impedances. Suppose that the admittance of a load terminating a transmission is measured and it is found not to equal the line admittance. The load may be matched at one frequency by placing components of suitable susceptance across the line.

Suppose the load admittance is plotted on the circle diagram, Fig. 2.11. Transformation of this admittance along the line towards the generator corresponds to rotation in the clockwise direction. At some point the circle of constant reflection coefficient crosses the circle for $G = 1$ and at this point the conductance of the transformed load admittance is equal to that of the line. The susceptance of the load at this point can be read from the chart and if an equal susceptance of opposite sign is connected across the line, the load will be matched to the line so that there is no standing wave on the line.

The matching susceptance can be placed either at the distance from the load indicated on the circle diagram which will be within half a wavelength of the load or at multiples of a half wavelength further towards the generator. A position as near to the load as possible should be chosen to minimize the frequency sensitivity of the system.

In an adjustable matching system, it is often not convenient to move the matching susceptance along the line. In this case, two susceptances may be used spaced a quarter of a wavelength apart, for example two short circuit sections of transmission line. Such a twin stub tuning unit will compensate for many but not all values of mismatch. The operation of the matching unit can be explained by reference to the circle diagram, Fig. 2.11. Suppose that the load admittance transformed to the position of the matching line nearest the load is plotted at A, a normalized admittance of $(0·3 + j0·5)$. A variable susceptance in parallel leaves the conductance unchanged but the total susceptance can be varied to any desired value B, the total admittance lying still on the $G = 0·3$ circle. The total susceptance transformed to the position of the second variable susceptance, a quarter of a wavelength further down the line, is found by drawing a line through the centre point $R = 1$. The transformed susceptance is diametrically opposite B at B'. For achieving a match B' should lie on the $R = 1$ circle. The first susceptance and hence the position B is adjusted to achieve this. As B' then lies on the $R = 1$ circle, the second susceptance can be used to cancel the remaining mismatch. It is clear from this construction that if the initial value of admittance A has a conductance greater than unity, the position of A lies within the $R = 1$ circle and the resulting mismatch cannot be corrected. In such a case, if the matching unit can be moved a further quarter wavelength from the load, the new transformed value of A lies outside the $R = 1$ circle and the mismatch can be corrected. As an alternative to moving the matching section, a third shunt line may be used a further quarter wavelength along the guide or a phase shifter may be included in the main transmission line.

CHAPTER 3

Matrix Theory of Microwave Components

Many microwave problems can be treated by using the one dimensional equivalent circuit treatment. Having reduced the microwave system to a series of equivalent lumped components connected by transmission lines it is natural to use a circuit matrix treatment for the resulting equivalent circuit. This approach can be very useful when fairly complicated microwave circuits are involved and it is usually easier to derive the properties and limitations of the system from this method than from electromagnetic theory. Furthermore it is quite easy to include non-reciprocal components in the matrix treatment.

Consider any passive linear n-port junction in waveguide, stripline or co-axial cable where the plane of the ports has been chosen so that only the dominant mode exists for the particular transmission line under consideration. If the ports are labelled 1 to n and the equivalent transmission line currents and voltages are $V_1, I_1 \ldots V_n I_n$ then the circuit equations have the normal form

$$V_1 = Z_{11}I_1 + Z_{12}I_2 + \ldots Z_{1n}I_n$$
$$V_2 = Z_2I_1 + Z_{22}I_2 + \ldots Z_{2n}I_n$$
$$\cdots \cdots \cdots \cdots \cdots$$
$$V_n = Z_{n1}I_1 + Z_{n2}I_2 + \ldots Z_{nn}I_n$$

The system is assumed to be linear and passive and the impedances Z_{mn} give the component of the voltage at port m caused by a unit current at port n.

It is usual to write the properties of the n-port junction as an impedance matrix

$$[Z] = \begin{bmatrix} Z_{11} & Z_{12} \ldots Z_{1n} \\ Z_{21} & Z_{22} \ldots Z_{2n} \\ \cdot & \cdot \quad \cdot \\ Z_{n1} & Z_{n2} \ldots Z_{nn} \end{bmatrix}$$

In the case of reciprocal devices, which implies that the junction is filled with a uniform isotropic medium, then the matrix is symmetrical, that is $Z_{ij} = Z_{ji}$. For loss free devices $Re(Z_{ij}) = 0$ also.

Thus all the terms Z_{ij} must be imaginary. This arises because any lossless network must be composed of pure reactances and Z_{ij} gives the voltage produce at port i (when it is an open circuit) for a unit current at port j. As the network is entirely reactive the voltage produced at port m must be exactly in quadrature with the impressed current.

Alternatively the admittance matrix may be used

$$[Y] = \begin{bmatrix} Y_{11} & Y_{12} \ldots Y_{1n} \\ Y_{21} & Y_{22} \ldots Y_{2n} \\ \cdot & \cdot \quad \cdot \quad \cdot \\ Y_{n1} & Y_{n2} \ldots Y_{nn} \end{bmatrix}$$

Again for a reciprocal device $Y_{ij} = Y_{ji}$ and for a lossless system $Re(Y_{ij}) = 0$.

Voltages and currents are seldom measured in microwave systems so that the impedance and admittance matrices are of limited use. However, the ratios of reflected to transmitted voltages, currents, or fields, at the various ports are of great interest and it is these ratios that are commonly measured. Consider the output plane of port m of an n-port device and let the complex amplitudes of the incident and reflected electric fields at the plane be a_m and b_m respectively. The electric field may vary across the plane of the port and will be given by a function of the form

$$\mathrm{E}(x, y, z_m) = (a_m + b_m)e_m$$

where e_m is the electric field vector mode function of the transverse form for the dominant mode in the mth line. This function indicates the cross-sectional form of the electric field for the particular mode under consideration. In a similar manner the magnetic field is given by

$$\mathrm{H}(x, y, z_m) = (a_m - b_m)h_m$$

where h_m is the magnetic field vector mode function. The fields e_m and h_m are related by the characteristic impedance of the mth line, Z_{0m}. For convenience Z_{0m} is chosen so that the power flow into the junction is given by

$$P = \tfrac{1}{2} \mid a_m \mid^2 - \tfrac{1}{2} \mid b_m \mid^2$$

We now relate the various a and b coefficients by a series of scattering coefficients. Thus S_{11} is the ratio of the complex amplitudes of the end incident waves at port 1, i.e.

$$b_1 = S_{11}a_1$$

The reflected waves at the other ports due to the signal at the first port are given by

$$b_2 = S_{21}a_1$$
$$b_3 = S_{31}a_1$$
$$b_n = S_{n1}a_1$$

(The 'reflected' wave at the other ports is the wave travelling away from the junction, and if the junction is excited at one port only it is not strictly speaking 'reflected' but is referred to thus.) If there is a wave incident at port 2 then there is a second set of equations

$$b_1 = S_{12}a_2$$
$$b_2 = S_{22}a_2$$
$$b_n = S_{n2}a_n$$

As only linear systems are being considered, the total amplitude of the wave travelling away from any port is the sum of the waves caused by the waves incident on all the separate ports so the complete set of equations has the form

$$b_1 = S_{11}a_1 + S_{12}a_2 \ldots + S_{1n}a_n$$
$$b_2 = S_{21}a_1 + S_{22}a_2 \ldots + S_{2n}a_n$$
$$\cdot \quad \cdot \quad \cdot \quad \cdot \quad \cdot \quad \cdot \quad \cdot \quad \cdot$$
$$b_n = S_{n1}a_1 + S_{n2}a_2 \ldots s_{nn}a_n$$

The scattering matrix of this set of equations is

$$[S] = \begin{bmatrix} S_{11} + S_{12} \ldots S_{1n} \\ S_{21} + S_{22} \ldots S_{2n} \\ S_{n1} + S_{n2} \ldots S_{nn} \end{bmatrix} \text{ and } b = [S]a$$

This type of matrix has a number of advantages compared with the impedance or admittance matrix. Firstly the coefficients can readily be measured thus. If all but one port is terminated in its matched load then the reflection coefficient at the remaining port, say the mth port, is S_{kk}. Also the ratio of the power emerging from port k when a signal is applied to port i only may be used to find S_{ik}.

Another advantage is that the various ports need not be lines of the same impedance, or even the same form. Furthermore, changing the plane of the port changes the *phase* of the scattering coefficient so that plane of the ports may be chosen such that the phase shift is zero and then the scattering coefficient reduced to real numbers.

This simplification is not possible in the case of impedance or admittance matrices.

There are two special types of scattering matrices to be considered. Firstly if the device being considered is reciprocal, that is the medium within it is uniform and isotropic, then the matrix is symmetrical and $S_{ij} = S_{ji}$. Secondly if the junction is lossless the total sum of the powers entering it must be zero. As the coefficients a and b have been normalized to the impedances of the various lines the power entering the junction at the ith port is given by

$$P_{in} = \tfrac{1}{2}a_i a_i{}^* - \tfrac{1}{2}b_i b_i{}^*$$

and the sum of these powers for all ports must be zero. This condition can only be satisfied if the matrix is unitary, that is

$$\widetilde{S}{}^* = S^{-1}$$

which may also be written as

$$\widetilde{S}{}^* S = I$$

$\widetilde{S}{}^*$ is the transpose of the complex conjugate of S (Hermitian adjoint) and I is the unit matrix. In terms of the individual elements of the matrix this means that

$$S_{ki} S_{kj}{}^* = \delta_{ij}$$

where δ_{ij} is

1 if $i = j$

0 if $i \neq j$

The unitary condition may be checked very easily as the above conditions imply that the product of any column of the matrix with the complex conjugate of that same column is unity whilst the product of any column with the complex conjugate of any other column is zero.

In the special case of a reciprocal device having a symmetrical matrix the transpose is equal to the matrix and the unitary condition reduces to

$$S^* S = I$$

The application of these rules to a number of possible microwave junctions will now be considered.

One port device

The scattering 'matrix' consists only of one element which is the reflection coefficient for the component.

<hr>

* Indicates the complex conjugate.

Two port devices

The scattering matrix has the general form

$$[S] = \begin{bmatrix} S_{11} & S_{12} \\ S_{21} & S_{22} \end{bmatrix}$$

For the reciprocal devices the matrix will be symmetrical and $S_{12} = S_{21}$.

If the device is to be matched at both ports then both S_{11} and S_{22} will be zero. Thus a simple lossless section of transmission line has the matrix

$$[S] = \begin{bmatrix} 0 & e^{j\theta} \\ e^{j\theta} & 0 \end{bmatrix}$$

where θ is the phase change on transmission.

A perfect lossless isolator that allows power to pass in one direction unattenuated but absorbs all the power flowing in the opposite direction has the matrix

$$[S] = \begin{bmatrix} 0 & 0 \\ e^{j\theta} & 0 \end{bmatrix}$$

By altering the position of the plane of the ports to give zero phase shift the matrices of the two devices just considered become

$$[S] = \begin{bmatrix} 0 & 1 \\ 1 & 0 \end{bmatrix}$$

for the reciprocal device and

$$[S] = \begin{bmatrix} 0 & 0 \\ 1 & 0 \end{bmatrix}$$

for the non-reciprocal one.

If the unitary condition is applied it will not be satisfied by the matrix of the non-reciprocal device indicating that a lossless two port isolator is not possible. With such a simple device this fact is obvious from simple consideration, but for more complex devices this form of check on the properties of the component can be very valuable.

Three port devices

The general form of the matrix is

$$[S] = \begin{bmatrix} S_{11} & S_{12} & S_{13} \\ S_{21} & S_{22} & S_{23} \\ S_{31} & S_{32} & S_{33} \end{bmatrix}$$

If the device is to be matched at all three ports then the major diagonal terms of the matrix must be zero. If a reciprocal three port system is considered then the matrix becomes

$$[S] = \begin{bmatrix} 0 & S_{12} & S_{13} \\ S_{12} & 0 & S_{23} \\ S_{13} & S_{23} & 0 \end{bmatrix}$$

If the device is also to be lossless then the unitary conditions require

$$S_{12}S_{12}{}^* + S_{13}S_{13}{}^* = 1 \qquad S_{13}S_{23}{}^* = 0$$
$$S_{12}S_{12}{}^* + S_{23}S_{23}{}^* = 1 \qquad S_{12}S_{23}{}^* = 0$$
$$S_{13}S_{13}{}^* + S_{23}S_{23}{}^* = 1 \qquad S_{12}S_{13}{}^* = 0$$

The second set of conditions for the unitary matrix require that either one or other of the two terms in each of these equations is zero, that is two of the three scattering terms must be zero. However if this condition is applied to the first set of equations it is not possible to satisfy them. In fact it is found that it is only possible to satisfy the unitary conditions if one of the major diagonal terms is unity. This means that one of the three ports is isolated from any outside source. Thus any *lossless* reciprocal three port device cannot be matched simultaneously at all three ports.

A simple example is a lossless waveguide tee junction. The H plane junction of Fig. 6.1 will be examined. From symmetry it is apparent that

$$S_{11} = S_{22}$$
$$S_{13} = S_{23}$$

We have already seen that only two ports can be matched so let ports 1 and 2 be matched, i.e.

$$S_{11} = S_{22} = 0$$

The requirement of a unitary matrix implies that

$$S_{12}S_{12}{}^* + S_{13}S_{13}{}^* = 1 \qquad S_{13}S_{13}{}^* = 0$$
$$2S_{13}S_{13}{}^* + S_{33}S_{33}{}^* = 1 \qquad S_{12}S_{13}{}^* + S_{13}S_{33}{}^* = 0$$

Obviously S_{13} is zero and S_{33} and S_{12} unity so the only possible matrix is

$$[S] = \begin{bmatrix} 0 & 1 & 0 \\ 1 & 0 & 0 \\ 0 & 0 & 1 \end{bmatrix}$$

Arm three is thus isolated and can only be terminated by a perfectly reflecting piston.

Alternatively if port 3 is to be matched it is found that the matrix must have the form

$$[S] = \tfrac{1}{2} \begin{bmatrix} -1 & 1 & \sqrt{2} \\ 1 & -1 & \sqrt{2} \\ \sqrt{2} & \sqrt{2} & 0 \end{bmatrix}$$

The fact of $1/\sqrt{2}$ implies a 3 db split in the power which is obvious from physical symmetry also. The matrix gives further information which is not quite so obvious from simple considerations. For instance if power is incident on port 1 it is transmitted to port 3 with a 3 db drop, to port 2 with a 6 db drop, the remaining quarter of the power being reflected at port 1.

Consider now the non-reciprocal lossless three port junction. It is now possible to set all the three major diagonal components of the matrix to zero and still satisfy the unitary condition. A simple example is that of a physically symmetrical lossless non-reciprocal three port. Due to the physical symmetry we have

$$S_{12} = S_{23} = S_{31}$$

and

$$S_{21} = S_{32} = S_{13}$$

so the matrix has only two constants thus

$$[S] = \begin{bmatrix} 0 & S_{12} & S_{21} \\ S_{21} & 0 & S_{12} \\ S_{12} & S_{21} & 0 \end{bmatrix}$$

Application of the unitary condition yields

$$S_{12}S_{21}{}^* = 0$$

$$S_{21}S_{21}{}^* + S_{12}S_{12}{}^* = 1$$

$$S_{21}S_{12}{}^* = 0$$

thus either

$$S_{12} = 0, \quad S_{21} = 1$$

or

$$S_{21} = 0, \quad S_{12} = 1$$

and the corresponding two matrices are either

$$[S] = \begin{bmatrix} 0 & 0 & 1 \\ 1 & 0 & 0 \\ 0 & 1 & 0 \end{bmatrix}$$

or

$$[S] = \begin{bmatrix} 0 & 1 & 0 \\ 0 & 0 & 1 \\ 1 & 0 & 0 \end{bmatrix}$$

The first represents a circulator with a counterclockwise sense of rotation, the second one with a clockwise sense. In fact any lossless matched three port non-reciprocal device must conform to one of the above two matrices.

In the case of *lossy* three port devices simultaneous matching *is* possible.

Four port devices

In the case of reciprocal devices it is seen from Chapter 6 that a wide variety of physical arrangements are possible. The limitation that prevents simultaneous matching at all ports is not present in the case of a four port as the reader may conform by applying the unitary condition to a 4×4 symmetrical matrix with the major diagonal elements set to zero.

An ideal directional coupler is a good example of a lossless four port. Ports 1 and 2 are the main arms whilst 3 and 4 are the auxiliary arms. The coupler isolates port 4 from port 1 and port 3 from port 2. Thus the minor diagonal terms are zero also. From physical symmetry we assume that $S_{13} = S_{24}$. Thus the only constants are S_{12} and S_{13}. The unity conditions require that

$$S_{12}S_{12}{}^* + S_{13}S_{13}{}^* = 1, \ S_{34}S_{34}{}^* + S_{13}S_{13}{}^* = 1$$

The coupling factor between a main and the non-isolated auxiliary port may be anything from zero to unity and we will consider the case where one-half of the power is coupled to the auxiliary port, that is a 3 db coupler.

Thus S_{13} is $1/\sqrt{2}$ and from the unitary conditions S_{12} and S_{34} must also equal $1/\sqrt{2}$. The matrix is thus

$$[S] = \frac{1}{\sqrt{2}} \begin{bmatrix} 0 & 1 & 1 & 0 \\ 1 & 0 & 0 & 1 \\ 1 & 0 & 0 & 1 \\ 0 & 1 & 1 & 0 \end{bmatrix}$$

Another four port that may be considered in a simple manner is the magic tee junction. Physical symmetry shows that $S_{11} = S_{22}$ and that power into port 3 divides equally, and in phase, into ports 1 and 2. Power into port 4 divides equally, but in antiphase, into ports 1 and 2. Also the geometry is such that power into port 3 will not directly excite port 4 and vice versa. In a practical magic tee a matching arrangement is concluded so that port 3 is matched when all other ports are terminated in a matched load and similarly for port 4. The matrix can now be written down

$$[S] = \frac{1}{\sqrt{2}} \begin{bmatrix} 0 & 0 & 1 & 1 \\ 0 & 0 & -1 & 1 \\ 1 & -1 & 0 & 0 \\ 1 & 1 & 0 & 0 \end{bmatrix}$$

and will be found to satisfy the unitary condition also.

It must be remembered that in both the case of the directional coupler and the magic tee the practical devices are frequency sensitive and that the matrices are only applicable over a limited frequency range.

In the case of lossless non-reciprocal matched three port devices we have seen that only two matrices are possible. This restriction does not apply in the case of four port junctions. A fairly widely used four port non-reciprocal device is the circulator whose matrix is

$$[S] = \frac{1}{\sqrt{2}} \begin{bmatrix} 0 & 0 & 1 & 0 \\ 0 & 0 & 0 & 1 \\ 0 & 1 & 0 & 0 \\ 1 & 0 & 0 & 0 \end{bmatrix}$$

Device with more than four ports

The same methods may be applied to multi-port devices to examine their properties and limitations.

CHAPTER 4

Coupling and Matching of Transmission Systems

In any waveguide or co-axial line transmission system there are a number of different components which must be connected one with another, there are corners which must be turned and junctions to be made between different circuits. There are therefore a number of components which are necessary to complete any system which correspond to the connecting wires and connectors in low frequency systems. At microwave frequencies it is usually essential that these connecting pieces should maintain matched conditions through the system over a broad band of frequencies. The most elementary connecting device is that required to connect two similar co-axial lines or waveguides.

If the connector between two similar lines introduces a mismatch some of the incident power is reflected, causing a disturbance of the system. Also if the connector is part of a measuring system, and it is the properties of the part of the system beyond the connector which are of interest, it is important that the connector should not disturb

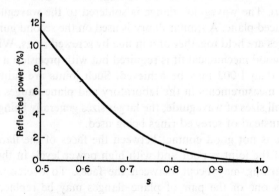

Figure 4.1. Reflection coefficient and reflected power.

the system. As the power reflection coefficient of a mismatch of v.s.w.r., s, is

$$R = \left(\frac{1-s}{1+s}\right)^2 \tag{4.1}$$

the percentage reflection of power may be calculated and is shown in Fig. 4.1. For precision measurements where accuracies of say 0.1% are required the power reflection due to the connector should be not greater than say 0.01% calling for a v.s.w.r. for the connector of better than 0.98.

Waveguide couplings

Waveguide couplings used for connecting sections of plain rectangular or cylindrical guide usually have to satisfy a number of design requirements. They must first of all provide a good electrical coupling over a range of frequencies for which the guide is to be used. They must also give a good mechanical joint and this may include being water and vacuum or pressure tight.

The electrical properties of the coupling must be such that the match is preserved and that the coupling is suitable at power levels up to the maximum that the guide will handle without breakdown. If a rectangular guide supporting the TE_{10} mode is considered, the lines of current flow in the waveguide walls are cut by a joint between two sections of waveguide. The coupling must therefore effectively join the two sections electrically. This may be achieved by a good butt joint between plane matching surfaces. The type of coupling joint that may be used at 3 cm wavelength with W.G. 16 is shown in Fig. 4.2(a). The waveguide flange is soldered to the waveguide and the end faced plane. A similar flange is used on the second guide. The two flanges are held together and in line by screwed rings. With such a joint a good mechanical fit is required but with precision a v.s.w.r. of better than 1.002 may be achieved. Such joints are suitable for precision measurements in the laboratory and plane flanges may be used for all sizes of waveguide, the larger sizes generally being bolted together instead of screwed rings being used.

If there is not good contact between the faces of the flanges the v.s.w.r. of the joint is poor and with high power levels in the waveguide sparking may occur between the faces. To overcome these difficulties one of the pair of plane flanges may be replaced by a choke flange as shown in Fig. 4.2(b), again for W.G. 16. If the section of a joint between a choke and a plane flange is examined it may be seen that the channel between the two flanges and into the choke flange forms a section of transmission line $\lambda/2$ in length with the end away from the waveguide terminated by a short circuit. The short circuit at the end of this section of line transforms to a short circuit at the plane between the two ends of the waveguides giving an electrical coupling between these points without the faces touching mechanically. The mechanical joint occurs at a point $\lambda/4$ from the

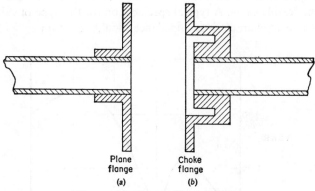

Plane
flange
(a)

Choke
flange
(b)

Figure 4.2. Waveguide couplings.

end of the short circuit section and at this point there is a minimum of current flow. There is therefore not the same necessity for a good mechanical fit at this point as there is if two plane flanges are to be used.

For systems which are to be water, pressure, or vacuum tight a channel may be cut in the flange to take an O-ring seal. When the two flanges are pulled together by the screwed rings or bolts the O-ring is compressed to form an effective seal. This type of choke coupling has a v.s.w.r. of better than 1·02 over the design range of frequencies.

Co-axial line couplings

The co-axial line coupling has to fulfil the same functions as the waveguide coupling but the design is complicated by the presence of the inner conductor and the necessity to support and join this conductor as well as the outer conductor. There are a number of designs of coupling in common use some of which are well matched over a wide band of frequencies and others which have been designed

E

to have a good match over a limited frequency range. The range of co-axial connectors has to be designed to fit with both rigid and flexible cables and separate designs have to be made for cables of differing characteristic impedance. The design of connectors is also dependent on whether there is a need for easy connection and disconnection or whether a more permanent connection is acceptable if a better match can be achieved.

Typical of the type of connector used with flexible co-axial cables is the type N connector. This connector is designed for use with 50 ohm flexible cable. A typical specification for this type of cable is that the mean characteristic impedance should lie within $2\frac{1}{2}\%$ of the

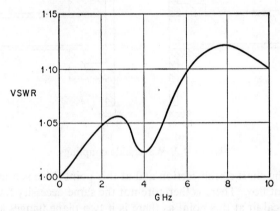

Figure 4.3. v.s.w.r. of a pair of type N connectors.

nominal impedance and that the standard deviation in impedance should be not more than 3%. If there is a step jump in impedance of 3% the v.s.w.r. on the cable due to this jump will be 0·97. This may be compared with the mismatch introduced by the connector. The v.s.w.r. introduced by the standard design is shown in Fig. 4.3, together with that of an improved design for which the v.s.w.r. is not greater than 0·98 over most of the design range of frequencies [1]. A precision connector however may be designed to have a v.s.w.r. of better than 0·999 and this type of connection may be required for precision measurements [2].

Whilst it is possible to construct co-axial connectors with a low residual mismatch, care must be taken when using normal commercial connectors with flexible cables. Large discontinuities may be introduced in the connector by faulty insertion of the cable in the connector.

The problem of making permanent interconnections between stripline components is not so likely to occur as the stripline form of construction is best suited to the production of integrated microwave systems, either as conventional printed circuits or as microstrip semi-conductor integrated circuits. A range of stripline components is commercially available in which a satisfactory connection is achieved by stepping and overlapping the conductors on adjacent components. Such a range of components is useful in experimental systems.

An interconnection between stripline and co-axial line is often required and both in-line and right-angle joints have been used. Some discontinuity is introduced at the transition but this may be minimized by reducing the physical dimensions of the transition. Thus, whilst transitions between type N connectors and stripline are satisfactory at frequencies up to about 3 GHz, giving a v.s.w.r. of about 0·98, at higher frequencies miniature connectors should be used. The match of the transition depends on the suppression of spurious modes. This may be achieved by a ring of screws around the transition on a radius of about half a wavelength.

Bends and junctions in waveguide

In waveguide systems the guide may be carried around corners either by a curved section of waveguide or by some type of mitred corner. Even a gentle bend in a section of waveguide will introduce some mismatch into the system due to the disturbance of the field pattern in the bend. For circular bends the mismatch will depend on the radius of the bend and on the plane of the bend. The bends are known as E plane or H plane bends and the two types are illustrated in Fig. 4.4. There is an optimum radius for the bend and this occurs when the bend length is a multiple of half the guide wavelength. Bends of this type have a v.s.w.r. of better than 0·95.

The alternative method of using a mitred corner is illustrated in Fig. 4.5. These corners have the advantage of being compact but, at the discontinuity formed by the corner, a mismatch will occur. The effect of the mismatch may be reduced by using a double mitre corner. Each change in direction introduces a discontinuity but if these are placed $\lambda_g/2$ apart their effect will cancel at that particular wavelength. The mismatch may also be minimized by using a

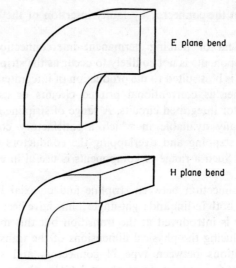

Figure 4.4. Waveguide bends.

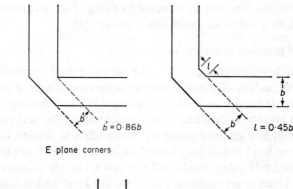

$b' = 0.86b$ $l = 0.45b$

E plane corners

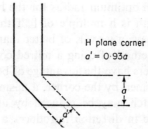

H plane corner
$a' = 0.93a$

Figure 4.5. Waveguide corners.

suitably positioned corner plate. Typical dimensions are shown in Fig. 4.6. The bandwidth of this type of corner may be increased by increasing the number of discrete steps. A corner with three changes in direction may be designed to have a bandwidth of 10%.

In rectangular waveguide systems it may be necessary to change the plane of the waveguide along the run using some kind of twist or transition. The simple twist in waveguide performs best when the length of the twist is equal to some multiple of half the guide wavelength. For twists of length about $3\lambda_g$ the residual v.s.w.r. may be better than 0·95. If the plane of the guide is to be rotated over a shorter distance it may be better to use a stepped transition, Fig. 4.6. This consists of a number of quarter wavelength sections of guide. The v.s.w.r. of the transition improves with the number of sections. With three sections a residual v.s.w.r. of better than 0·95 may be achieved over a 10% bandwidth.

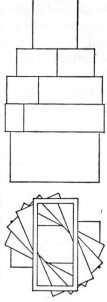

Figure 4.6. Waveguide twist.

Adjustable matching units

In many microwave circuits it is convenient to be able to introduce adjustable matching units to cancel out the mismatch which may exist in other circuit components. Such adjustable matching units may be constructed from, either, short circuited sections of transmission line connected in series or parallel with the main line, or variable reactances. The short circuit section of line may be used in either co-axial line or waveguide. The reactance at the terminals of the short circuit section may take any positive or negative value.

A load on the main transmission line will present a certain value of admittance at the plane of the short-circuit line. The imaginary part of the admittance may be varied by the addition of reactance by the short circuit section. A second short circuit section spaced $\lambda_g/4$ from the first section will present a reactance across the line at its own terminal plane but when this reactance is transformed along the transmission line to the plane of the first short circuit it will appear at that plane to provide a variable resistive admittance. Thus the two short circuit sections taken together can be used to provide any value of admittance across the main transmission line. This adjustable admittance taken in parallel with the load admittance may be adjusted to give a match. This matching process may be illustrated diagramatically as shown in Fig. 4.7. At the plane of one short circuit, that short circuit will give adjustment along the imaginary axis while the second short circuit will give adjustment along the real axis. If at the reference plane the load on the main transmission line has a normalized admittance $(A + jB)$ the value of the two short circuits

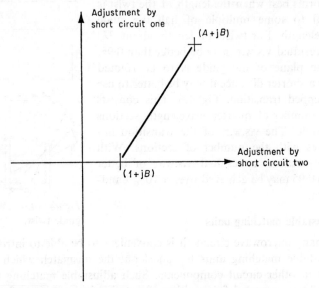

Figure 4.7. Matching diagram.

can be adjusted to $(1 - A - jB)$ to give a resultant normalized admittance of unity.

A similar adjustment process may be carried out using screw matching sections. If a screw is inserted through the broad wall of a waveguide it will introduce a capacitance across the guide at that plane. A second screw spaced $\lambda_g/4$ away will again introduce a capacitance or positive imaginary admittance on its own plane but when this admittance is transformed through a quarter wavelength it gives negative imaginary admittance. A further pair of screws placed at $\lambda_g/8$ and $3\lambda_g/8$ from the first screw will introduce positive and negative real admittance at the plane of the first screw so that in this plane the four screws can introduce a value of admittance, positive or negative, real or imaginary.

To match any particular admittance $(A + jB)$ only two screws need be used to give $(1 - A - jB)$. For another load such as $(-A - jB)$ another pair of the screws will be needed to give the value of $(1 + A + jB)$ required for matching. The adjustment of such a matching unit is relatively simple as the variation of real and imaginary parts is independent. Another type of screw matching section uses screws placed $3\lambda_g/8$ apart. The three screws can introduce between them any value of admittance but the adjustment of the screw is no longer independent as it now takes place along three axes at $120°$ instead of four axes at $90°$.

Another type of matching unit used in waveguide is the $E - H$ tuning section. This consists of two short circuit sections, one connected into the broad wall of the waveguide and the second in the narrow wall in a similar way to a magic T. One arm provides a parallel reactance, the second a series reactance. If the load in the plane of the tuner is $(R + jX)$ then this combined with a series reactance of jA, gives a total load of $[R + j(X + A)]$. This corresponds to an admittance of

$$\frac{R - j(X + A)}{R^2 + (X + A)^2}$$

This admittance taken in parallel with a susceptance jB is

$$\frac{R - j(X + A - B)}{R^2 + (X + A)^2}$$

By adjusting the values of A and B any required admittance may be achieved.

All these matching devices depend on spacings which are frequency sensitive and are narrow band devices. To achieve a broad band match the components of the circuit must all be individually matched over a broad band and these narrow band matching devices cannot be relied on.

Matched loads

Another essential component in microwave circuits is the matched load. The matched load absorbs all the incident power and dissipates this power as heat. The design of the load depends on the incident power level and the type of guide structure. At low power levels the dissipative element may consist of resistive card or a plastic material loaded with dissipative material, typically an epoxy resin loaded with carbonyl iron powder. This type of load is tapered across the guide section to reduce reflection of power. The power handling capacity depends on the rise in temperature in the load. For high power levels a water load may be used, Fig. 4.8. In waveguide this may consist of a pyrex tube mounted across the waveguide usually along a tapered

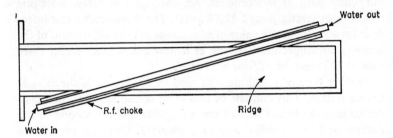

Figure 4.8. Matched load.

ridge in the guide. Water is circulated through the tube to remove the heat.

To ensure that little reflection occurs from the load it is important to prevent bubbles forming in the water. These may occur if there are stagnant points in the water and the power incident on the load is high. This problem is more likely to occur with co-axial line loads because of the difficulty of ensuring good water flow at the point at which the water load tapers to the centre conductor. A water load such as this may be used as a water calorimeter to measure the incident power using a continuous flow method of heat measurement.

References

[1] S. B. Cohn, *The Co-axial Connector Revolution, Microwave Journal,* 1964, Vol. 7, No. 10, p. 16.
[2] D. Woods, *A Co-axial Connector System for Precision r.f. Measuring Instruments and Standards, P.I.E.E.,* 1961, **108B**, 205.

CHAPTER 5

One and Two Port Devices

One port devices are the short circuit section of line, the matched load, and controllable mismatch sections. Matched loads have been described in Chapter 4, together with the use of short circuit sections of line. The construction of adjustable short circuit sections may be classified according to whether the movable plunger makes electrical contact with the guide walls or not. If contact is made with the walls some kind of spring finger contact is used to try and ensure a good electrical contact in a known position. Good contact is necessary as the short circuit position is a position of maximum current flow and minimum voltage. The reliability of a contacting short circuit plunger may be improved by having the point of contact displaced from the short circuit plane by using a recessed plunger, Fig. 5.1(a). The short circuit plane and position of maximum current flow is now within the plunger and the contact position is no longer at the voltage minimum. If the contact of the contact fingers is poor the precise short circuit position may be uncertain and may vary relative to the plunger with movement of the plunger.

A better type of plunger to use in measuring systems is the non-contacting plunger. This is illustrated in Fig. 5.1(b). The gap between the plunger and the guide walls may be filled with p.t.f.e. for easy movement and to locate the plunger. The variation in the spacing between plunger and the guide walls forms alternate sections of transmission line of low and high impedance. At each change of impedance there is a large mismatch, for example if at the first mismatch 90% of the incident power is reflected, then 10% is transmitted to the second mismatch, where if again 90% of the incident power is reflected, the transmitted power is only 1% of the total and only 0·1% at a third mismatch. By spacing the mismatch positions by $\lambda_g/4$ the reflected components all add in phase to achieve near 100% reflection.

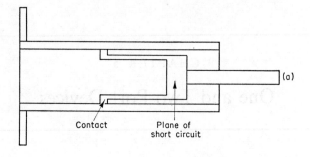

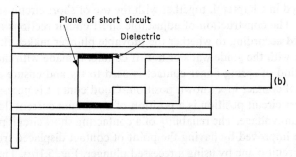

Figure 5.1. Short circuit plungers.

Reciprocal two port waveguide devices

Reciprocal two port waveguide devices have the same properties for signals travelling through the device in either direction. Examples of reciprocal devices are waveguides containing posts or irises and waveguide and co-axial filters. Non-reciprocal devices may be made which have different properties for signals travelling through the device in the two opposite directions. Passive non-reciprocal devices can for example be made using the properties of ferrite materials.

In Chapter 3 the matrix treatment of discontinuities is considered. The scattering matrix of a discontinuity gives one method of describing the properties of a device as they appear to the external circuit and as they may be found from external measurements. A waveguide or other transmission line discontinuity may also be described in terms of a T or π section of line in which the impedances of the T or π depend on the form of the discontinuity. For loss free discontinuities the T or π has purely reactive impedances. For obstacles which are transverse to the direction of propagation and which have no finite length along the guide the T or π section reduces to a shunt reactance, the series components being zero.

Various methods may be used to calculate the impedance presented by an obstacle. Usually some kind of approximate method must be used in these calculations as the boundary conditions imposed on the field equations by the presence of the obstacle make an analytic solution difficult. The approximate methods employed are those using a series expansion of the field in a number of modes which are chosen to satisfy the boundary conditions [1], those using a variational technique [2] and those using finite difference methods [3].

For a waveguide which supports only the dominant mode the effect of a discontinuity may be represented by the reflection coefficient and the transmission coefficient of the discontinuity. If the modulus and phase angle of the reflection coefficient are $|\rho|$ and θ and for the transmission coefficient are $|\tau|$ and ϕ then from the conservation of energy

$$\tau\tau^* = 1 - |\rho|^2 \tag{5.1}$$

provided that the discontinuity is loss free. The effective impedance of the discontinuity may be derived from the transmission and reflection coefficients and these coefficients may be found knowing the fields set up in the guide. These coefficients may also be measured and the impedance of the discontinuity derived from the measured values.

The fields in a waveguide may be determined from wave equations of the form

$$(\nabla_t^2 + k^2)\phi = 0 \tag{5.2}$$

subject to the boundary conditions. In a uniform guide the ϕ term in the wave equation may describe the longitudinal H field, H_z for TE modes, or the longitudinal E field, E_z, for TM modes. The factor k is an eigen-value or characteristic value which depends on the mode considered and ∇_t^2 is the Laplacian operator for the transverse field.

For TE_{m0} modes in a rectangular guide expansion of the wave equation gives

$$\frac{\partial^2 E_y}{\partial x^2} + \frac{\partial^2 E_y^2}{\partial z^2} + k^2 E_y = 0 \tag{5.3}$$

which with the equations

$$j\omega\mu_0 H_z = -\frac{\partial E_y}{\partial x}$$

$$j\omega\mu_0 H_x = \frac{\partial E_y}{\partial z}$$

(5.4)

determines the field.

These equations have a solution

$$E_y = \sin\left(\frac{m\pi x}{a}\right)e^{\mp\gamma mz}$$

$$H_x = \mp\frac{\gamma_m}{jZ_0 k}\sin\left(\frac{m\pi x}{a}\right)e^{\mp\gamma mz}$$

$$H_z = \frac{jm\pi}{aZ_0 k}\cos\left(\frac{mnx}{a}\right)e^{\mp\gamma mz}$$

(5.5)

where

$$\gamma_m{}^2 = \left(\frac{m\pi}{a}\right)^2 - k^2 \tag{5.6}$$

and Z_0 is the wave impedance of free space.

When the wave propagates, γ_m is imaginary and the wave impedance E_y/H_x is real. When the wave is evanescent, the wave impedance is imaginary.

Suppose a wave of amplitude a_1 is incident on to a discontinuity. The discontinuity will set up a reflected wave of amplitude $R_1 a_1$ in the incident mode and also an infinite number of higher order modes. In the region $z \leqslant 0$, the incident field side of the discontinuity, the total transverse field may be written

$$E_y = a_1(e^{-\gamma_1 z} + R_1 e^{\gamma_1 z})\phi_1 + \sum_2^\infty a_n\phi_n e^{\gamma mz}$$

$$H_x = -\gamma_1 a_1(e^{-\gamma_1 z} - R_1 e^{\gamma_1 z})\phi_1 + \sum_2^\infty a_m\phi_m e^{\gamma mz}$$

(5.7)

where

$$\phi_m = \left(\frac{2}{a}\right)\sin\left(\frac{m\pi x}{a}\right) \tag{5.8}$$

For a waveguide which will only support the dominant mode, at some distance d from the discontinuity, only the first terms in the field series expansions will be significant and then

$$Z_{in} = \frac{E_y}{H_x} = \frac{(e^{-\gamma_1 d} + R_1 e^{\gamma_1 d})}{(e^{-\gamma_1 d} - R_1 e^{\gamma_1 d})}Z_1 \tag{5.9}$$

where Z_1 is the wave impedance of the uniform guide and Z_{in} is the wave impedance of the disturbed guide.

Writing

$$Z_{in} = Z_1 \cdot \frac{Z_L + jZ_1 \tan \beta_1 d}{Z_1 + jZ_L \tan \beta_1 d} \qquad (5.10)$$

the normal transmission line expression, the effective impedance of the discontinuity at the plane $z = 0$ is given by

$$Z_L = \frac{1 + R_1}{1 - R_1} Z_1 \qquad (5.11)$$

The normalized impedance of the discontinuity is thus

$$\frac{Z_L}{Z_1} = \frac{1 + R_1}{1 - R_1} \qquad (5.12)$$

For the region $z \geqslant 0$, beyond the discontinuity,

$$\left. \begin{array}{l} E_y = \displaystyle\sum_{n=1}^{\infty} b_n \psi_n e^{-\gamma n z} \\[3ex] H_z = \displaystyle\sum_{n=1}^{\infty} b_n \gamma_{0n} \psi_n e^{-\gamma n z} \end{array} \right\} (5.13)$$

Again assume that only the dominant mode propagates, i.e. the mode for which $n = 1$. Then γ_n is imaginary and γ_{0n} is real. At the discontinuity the transverse fields must be continuous so

$$\left. \begin{array}{l} (a_1 + R_1)\phi_1 + \displaystyle\sum_{m=2}^{\infty} a_m \phi_m = \sum_{n=1}^{\infty} b_n \varphi_n \\[3ex] (a_1 - R_1)\gamma_1 \phi_1 - \displaystyle\sum_{m=2}^{\infty} a_m \gamma_m \phi_m = \sum_{n=1}^{\infty} b_n \gamma_{0n} \varphi_n \end{array} \right\} (5.14)$$

In theory these equations may be solved for given boundary conditions, in practice approximate methods must be used. For the more commonly used reactive elements, steps, irises and posts, tables are available showing the values of reactance produced by the discontinuities [4].

Practical forms of discontinuity

In waveguide systems discontinuities may be introduced into the system by changes in the waveguide dimensions, by inserting diaphragms across part of the waveguide, or by placing rods or posts across the guide. Some of these forms of discontinuity are illustrated in Fig. 5.2 together with their transmission line equivalent circuits. If the form of the discontinuity is such as to vary the electric field distribution the equivalent circuit is capacitive whilst if the discontinuity is such as to alter the magnetic field pattern the discontinuity appears

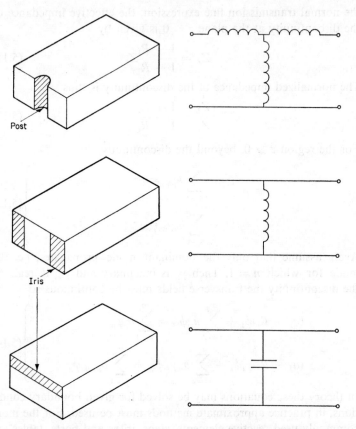

Figure 5.2. Forms of reactive discontinuity.

inductive. For example the posts illustrated have an inductive reactance while the diaphragms may be either inductive or capacitive depending on which waveguide dimension is restricted. If a diaphragm restricts both dimensions it will act as a resonant circuit. If the discontinuity has little length along the guide it will appear to be nearly a pure parallel reactance. If the discontinuity extends along the guide for an appreciable part of a wavelength the equivalent circuit is a Tee or π circuit with series components.

The actual values of impedance presented by discontinuities may be calculated or found from published tables. The values of impedance so obtained are for a single isolated obstacle remote from any other discontinuity. Each discontinuity sets up modes in the guide other than the normal mode of transmission. If the guide is operated in its principal mode these other modes will be evanescent along the guide but if two obstacles are placed close to each other the evanescent fields will interact and the effective impedance of the two obstacles taken together will differ from the value calculated from their isolated reactances.

Mode transducers

In many microwave systems different types of waveguides supporting different modes of propagation must be used. To convert from one guided mode to another mode, mode transducers are used. The mode transducer must be designed to set up the required electro-magnetic field configuration in the waveguide being fed with minimum loss,

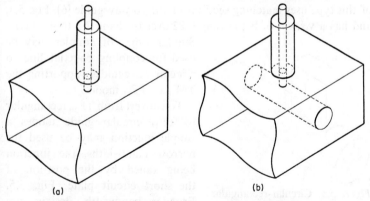

Figure 5.3. Waveguide-co-axial line transformers.

maximum bandwidth, and maximum power handling capacity. A compromise may have to be made between these factors to achieve a satisfactory design for a given application.

A type of transducer which is often required is a co-axial line TEM mode to TE_{10} rectangular mode transducer [5]. This may consist of a simple probe terminating the co-axial line in the waveguide, Fig. 5.3(a). This will set up the required field patterns, but is a narrow band device, and has a limited power handling capacity because of the high electric field strengths set up around the small probe. A transducer with a wider bandwidth is the bar and post coupler, Fig. 5.3(b). This design has a bar across the waveguide and the inner of the co-axial line is extended to the bar. The v.s.w.r. of the coupler is dependent on the dimensions of the bar and post and irises may be included in the design to improve the match. It is also possible

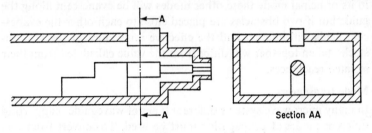

Figure 5.4. Ridge waveguide-co-axial line transformer.

to set up the required field pattern using a magnetic loop coupling in the end plate short-circuiting the waveguide. A developed design of this type uses matching sections of ridged waveguide [6], Fig. 5.4, and has a v.s.w.r. of better than 0·82 over the band 2·5 to 4·1 GHz.

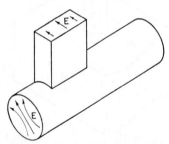

Figure 5.5. Circular-rectangular waveguide junction.

Similar types of coupler may be used for coupling co-axial line to circular waveguides supporting the TM_{10} or TE_{11} modes.

To convert from TE_{10} rectangular to TE_{11} circular guide modes a simple junction may be used for narrow bandwidths, the junction being tuned by the position of the short circuit plate, Fig. 5.5. Broader bandwidth designs use matching irises in their design. By feeding into the circular guide with two rectangular guides, mutually perpendicular, two orthogonal modes may be set up in the circular guide. The two modes set up in this way are linearly polarized. The circular guide will also support circularly polarized wave modes. Such a mode may be set up by using the two rectangular guide feeds, energized in such a way that if the two feeds are in the same plane along the circular guide, the feeds are in time quadrature. If the two feed points are displaced along the circular guide the relative feed phases must be adjusted. A second method of producing a circularly polarized wave is to use a dielectric polarizing plate in the waveguide. The circular waveguide is fed from the rectangular guide which sets up a linearly polarized wave in the circular waveguide. This wave may be considered to consist of two linearly polarized components each at 45° to the first wave. If now a dielectric plate is inserted into the circular guide parallel to one of these components it will delay the phase of that component relative to the phase of the component at right angles. If the relative delay is 90° a circularly polarized wave will be set up, Fig. 5.6.

Provided that the waveguides operate in their fundamental modes,

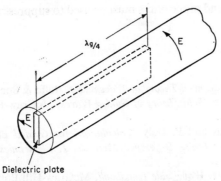

Figure 5.6. Linear to circular polarizer.

unwanted modes will not propagate. A more difficult problem is to make mode transducers for setting up higher order modes than the fundamental and for setting up only the one required mode. This requirement arises for instance when it is necessary to convert from an TE_{10} mode in a rectangular guide to an TE_{10} mode in a circular guide, the latter mode not being the fundamental mode in the circular guide. Several different mode transducers have been devised and some of these have been described by Karbowiak [7]. One type of coupler is shown in Fig. 5.7. This employs a gradual change in the guide cross-section to change from the rectangular to the circular cross-section. With suitable design this type of transducer can be made to operate over a large bandwidth. The second type of coupler depends on the velocities in two coupled guides for the modes of interest being the same. Energy is coupled from one guide to the

F

other through a series of coupling holes. If the voltage coupling co-efficient at each hole is c then there will be complete power transfer from one guide to the other if the coupling region is $k\pi/2c$ long,

Figure 5.7. TE$_{10}$ rectangular to TE$_{10}$ circular waveguide sector transducer.
(Reproduced by permission from A. E. Karbowiak, *Trunk Waveguide Communication*, Chapman & Hall.)

where k is an odd number. A difficulty may arise with this type of coupler if two modes with the same velocity can be supported by one of the guides. This occurs in circular guides with the TE$_{10}$ and the TM$_{11}$ modes, and mode filters must be used to suppress the unwanted mode.

References

[1] L. Lewin, *Advanced Theory of Waveguides*, Illiffe & Sons, 1951.
[2] R. E. Collins, *Field Theory of Guided Waves*, McGraw-Hill Book Co., 1960, p. 314.
[3] J. H. Collins and P. Daly, *Calculations for Guided Electromagnetic Waves Using Finite Difference Methods*, J. Electronics and Control, 1963, **14**, 361.
[4] N. Marcuvitz, *Waveguide Handbook*, McGraw-Hill Book Co., 1951.
[5] A. F. Harvey, *Microwave Engineering*, Academic Press, 1963, p. 101.
[6] J. C. Dix, *Design of Waveguide/Coaxial Transition for the Band*, 2·5–4·1 Gc/s, P.I.E.E., 1963, **110**, 253.
[7] A. E. Karbowiak, *Trunk Waveguide Communication*, Chapman and Hall Ltd., 1965.

CHAPTER 6

Multi-port Reciprocal Devices

A very wide variety of multi-port microwave reciprocal devices have been developed. Many of these were originally developed in waveguide but are now extensively used in stripline and co-axial form. The last two forms have been developed more recently and have the combined advantages of small size and weight, simpler constructional techniques and, in many cases, very wide bandwidths.

Simple three port junctions

Simple circuit theory, or the scattering matrix treatment of Chapter 3, shows that a lossless junction of three transmission systems of identical characteristic impedances cannot be simultaneously matched at all three ports. However such junctions are used for a number of purposes, particularly when one of the arms is to be terminated in a reactive load.

In co-axial cable and stripline the construction of the junction is quite simple and may take the form of a T or a Y. The stripline form lends itself to making an accurately symmetrical junction.

Three port waveguide junctions can take a variety of forms as the junction can be in the E plane or the H plane. Tee junctions in rectangular TE_{01} waveguide in the E and H planes are shown in Fig. 6.1 together with their equivalent circuit diagrams. These simplified circuit diagrams are correct for only one particular reference plane. It is seen that the choice of E or H plane results in a series or shunt junction, respectively.

Symmetrical 120° Y junctions may also be made and in Fig. 6.2 an E plane junction and its equivalent circuits are shown.

A 0° Y junction may be made by bifurcation of the guide as in Fig. 6.3. In the devices shown so far, the coupling aperture is the full cross-section of the guide, but slots or holes may be used for the coupling.

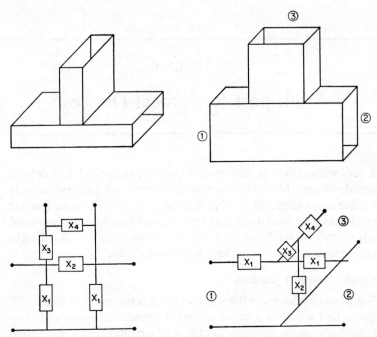

Figure 6.1. E and H plane waveguide junctions and their equivalent circuits.

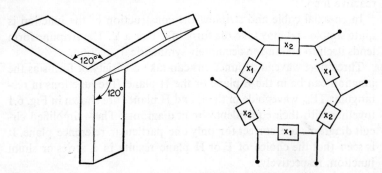

Figure 6.2. 120° E plane waveguide junction and its equivalent circuit.

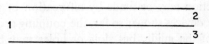

Figure 6.3. Bifurcated guide or 0° Y junction.

For obvious reasons these three port junctions are sometimes called power dividers.

Four port junctions

Hybrid junctions

This is a matched four port junction where power applied to one port splits equally to appear at two other ports, the fourth port being isolated. This may be achieved by connecting the four ports by lines of suitable lengths that cause the signals to add at two ports, but cancel at the fourth. A waveguide arrangement that achieves this is shown in Fig. 6.4(a). The frequency sensitivity of the device is mainly limited by the $3\lambda/2$ section. Similar devices can be made in co-axial

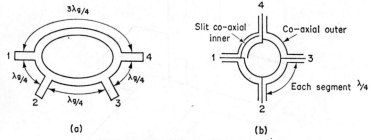

(a)   (b)

Figure 6.4(a). Waveguide hybrid ring.

Figure 6.4(b). Co-axial hybrid ring. The physical distance between each adjacent port is $\lambda/4$ but the section between ports 1 and 4 contains a split inner which gives a further 180° shift so that the electrical length of this particular section is $3\lambda/4$.

cable or stripline. For correct matching it is apparent that the impedance of the ring section must be $\sqrt{2}$ times the impedance of the connecting ports. In the former case the frequency sensitivity can be improved by replacing the $3\lambda/2$ line with a $\lambda/4$ line that has a split inner conductor as shown in Fig. 6.4(b). The distributed capacitance in the inner conductor introduces a 180° phase shift that is almost independent of frequency so the resulting device has a frequency response limited by only $\lambda/4$ line sections. Co-axial hybrids are used for many purposes, e.g. the balanced mixer system described in Chapter 10. The scattering matrix of a matched hybrid junction is

$$S = \frac{1}{\sqrt{2}} \begin{bmatrix} 0 & 1 & 0 & -1 \\ 1 & 0 & 1 & 0 \\ 0 & 1 & 0 & 1 \\ -1 & 0 & 1 & 0 \end{bmatrix}$$

(As usual the phase factor has been omitted. This would be actual matrix if each port arm were $\frac{3}{8}\lambda$ or $\frac{3}{8}\lambda_g$ in length)

The hybrid tee (magic tee) is shown in Fig. 6.5. Its properties can be determined by inspection. Any signal into port 1 will divide equally, and in phase, into ports 2 and 3. Also any signal into port 4 will divide equally, but in antiphase, into ports 2 and 3. Port 1 will not directly excite port 4 or vice versa. These properties arise due merely to the physical form of the device and its symmetry and are independent of frequency provided that it is within the pass band of the dominant mode of the guide. In the magic tee matching posts and

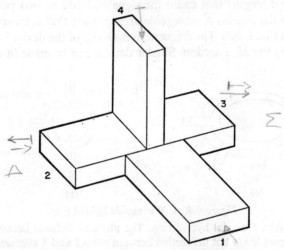

Figure 6.5. Magic tee hybrid junction.

diaphragms are introduced to ensure that any port appears matched if the other ports are terminated in a matched load. This matching does introduce a frequency sensitivity into the system.

The scattering matrix of a matched magic tee is given on p. 54.

A simple hybrid tee without the matching arrangement is often used in conjunction with two variable short circuiting pistons to form an E–H tuner.

By this means the variable reactances of the two short-circuited length of guide are placed in a series-parallel combination and the device can be used for matching out reflections in any system (see Chapter 4).

Directional couplers

A general description of a directional coupler is that it is a matched four port device in which a signal applied at any one port appears at two other ports, but not at the fourth. Thus the hybrid ring and the magic tee are both directional couplers. However in these two devices the input signal essentially divides in two. The device more generally referred to as a directional coupler is one in which the power can divide in almost any ratio between the two excited ports of the coupler. Such devices are made by introducing some form of coupling

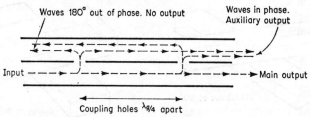

Figure 6.6. Basic principle of directional coupler. The dotted lines illustrate how the power divides at the coupling holes.

between two transmission lines. The coupling may occur at one discrete point along the length of the line, at several points or, particularly in the case of stripline systems, continuously. The basic principle of operation is the same as in the case of hybrid rings and magic tees, namely constructive or destructive combination of two or more signals at any given port which produces either an output, or in the destructive case, no output. A crude picture of the mechanism is given in Fig. 6.6 where a system using coupling at two points is used.

Waveguide couplers

The simplest waveguide coupler is shown in Fig. 6.7(a) and uses only one coupling hole. The interference pattern in the coupled guide is produced because both magnetic and electric field coupling is effective in this arrangement. A more common arrangement is that using two holes or two crosses (the Moreno cross coupler) as shown in Fig. 6.7(b). Another possible arrangement is to use two slots coupling the sidewalls of the guide (Fig. 6.7(c)). In all these simple arrangements the signal coupled into the secondary waveguide cannot be much less than about 15–20 db below that in the main guide. If closer coupling is required then multi-hole couplers must be used and only the configuration where the two guides run parallel is possible. The coupling can be made very large simply by using many holes. However as the holes have to be spaced $\lambda_g/4$ apart the bandwidth of the device is reduced if a number of holes are used.

The construction of multi-hole couplers at millimetre wavelengths presents some problems. One solution is to make the common wall of the waveguide a thin foil and to photo-etch the slots in the foil. The size and spacing of the slots can be very accurately controlled by this process.

Broadwall couplers, that is those in which the coupling slots are in

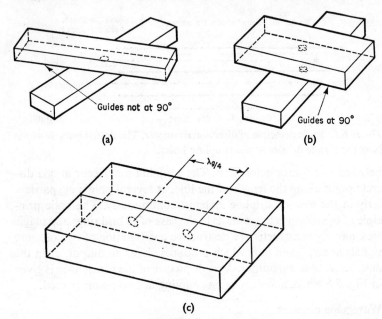

Guides not at 90°

(a)

Guides at 90°

(b)

λ_g/4

(c)

Figure 6.7. Waveguide couplers.

(a) Single hole coupler. The waveguides are at some angle other than 90°.

(b) Moreno cross couplers. The guides are at 90°.

(c) Two hole sidewall coupler.

the broad wall of the waveguide, may be made with very tight coupling, 3 db couplers being commercially available. They also have a high directivity (directivity being the ratio of signal coupled in one direction to that coupled in the other—in an ideal coupler no signal would be coupled in one direction) typical directivity being 30–40 db. However the power handling capacity of the broadwall coupler is very much less than that of the guide itself.

3 db directional couplers may be used as hybrid junctions in balanced mixer systems.

The sidewall coupler, where the coupling holes are in the narrow wall of the waveguide, has a higher power handling capacity, in some cases almost that of the waveguide itself. However, its directivity tends to be slightly inferior to that of the broadwall coupler, usually being about 25–30 db and the coupling of available devices does not usually exceed 10 db.

Branch line couplers

Branch line couplers consist of two transmission lines coupled through a number of branch lines, the length and spacing of the branch lines being a quarter wavelength at the mid-frequency. It will be noted that the waveguide couplers described earlier in this chapter are really a form of branch line coupler with almost zero branch line lengths.

In the case of waveguide systems the branch lines are usually in

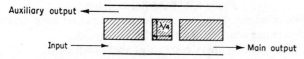

Figure 6.8. Branch line coupler. The two branch lines form E plane junctions with the two main guides. The branch lines are $\lambda/4$ apart and $\lambda/4$ in length.

series whilst in co-axial and stripline systems the branches are in parallel.

A simple branch line coupler using two quarter wave branch line is shown in Fig. 6.8.

Branch line couplers are not so common as other forms of directional coupler, but, in the waveguide version, they have the advantage that a high degree of coupling may be obtained in fairly short physical length.

Coupled transmission line directional couplers

If the fields of two TEM transmission lines are allowed to couple with each other, then, for suitable coupling lengths, a distributed directional coupler results. The simplest arrangement is to allow the distributed coupling to exist for a quarter wavelength as shown in Fig. 6.9(*a*). The coupled signal in the distributed coupler travels in the opposite direction to that of the input signal. Obviously, the device is only an ideal quarter wavelength at one frequency, but the coupling frequency response is approximately sinusoidal in shape and so the device has a fairly wide bandwidth.

In practice, the simplest physical form of coupler is that using two

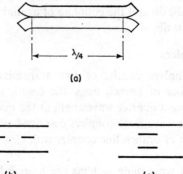

Figure 6.9. TEM line couplers.

(a) Basic principles. Two lines coupled over a quarter wave section.

(b) Triplate line coupling. Centre strips side by side.

(c) Triplate line coupling. Centre strips above each other.

striplines. Many forms of coupling may be used but configuration 6.9(*b*) is most used for weak coupling and 6.9(*c*) for tight coupling. A practical arrangement using configuration 6.9(*c*) is shown in Fig. 6.10. The coupler may be made either with the solid inner conductors

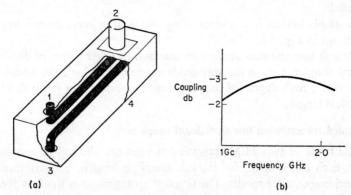

Figure 6.10. Quarter wave stripline coupler.

(a) Cutaway view of coupler showing two lines coupled over quarter-wave section. The ends of the striplines are coupled to co-axial sockets.

(b) Variation of coupling with frequency.

and air spacing or by using printed copper strips on dielectric boards, the microstrip technique. Typical variations in couplings, directivity and v.s.w.r. are shown in Fig. 6.10(b).

For simple quarter wave couplers the ratio of coupled voltage at port 3 to input voltage at port 1 is given by

$$\frac{V_3}{V_1} = \frac{j\,c\,\sin\theta}{\sqrt{(1-c^2)}\cos\theta + j\sin\theta} \qquad \text{where } c = \text{midband value of}$$

where c = midband value of V_3/V_1

θ = electrical length at coupler

Whilst the direct voltage at port 2 divided by the input voltage at port 1 is given by

$$\frac{E_2}{E_1} = \frac{\sqrt{(1-c^2)}}{\sqrt{(1-c^2)}\cos\theta + j\sin\theta}$$

the voltage at the fourth port being ideally zero at all frequencies. The very wide bandwidth of TEM systems makes it worthwhile attempting to increase the coupler bandwidth beyond that of the simple quarter wave device. A three quarter wave coupler has the response shown in Fig. 6.11(a) and consists of three individual couplers of different coupling factors, in cascade. By adjusting the coupling factors various responses can be obtained rather in the manner of filters using conventional lumped circuit elements. A printed circuit 3 db coupler having eight sections and giving an 8 : 1 bandwidth is shown in Fig. 6.11(c). On the same figure is the response of the coupler. Couplers with a bandwidth of up to 17 : 1 have been made by similar techniques.

It is convenient to make distributed couplers in stripline but to terminate the ends of the device in a stripline to co-axial transition, so that it may be connected in co-axial systems. These transitions have little effect on the performance at the lower frequencies but above a few GHz the transitions limit the performance of the couplers as their v.s.w.r. tends to deteriorate at higher frequencies.

Coupling of co-axial TEM lines is also possible but if tight coupling is required it is necessary to use the arrangement shown in Fig. 6.12(a). Here the coupling is enhanced by using a common outer conductor. However, this outer conductor cannot be connected directly to the outers of the cables connected to the four ports and has to be a floating quarter wave section as shown in the figure. Thus, although this is a co-axial coupler there are still problems in arranging the end connections so as to obtain a good match at the higher frequencies.

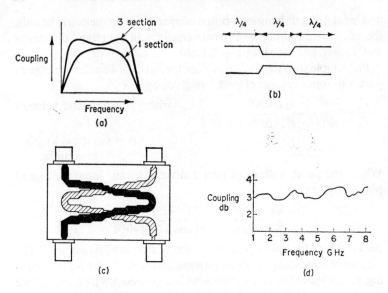

Figure 6.11.

(a) Coupling variation with frequency for single and three section couplers.

(b) Three quarter wave sections coupler.

(c) 8 : 1 Bandwidth 3 db coupler. Top and bottom covers (not shown) form the ground plates of the triplate system.

(d) Coupling variation with frequency for 8 : 1 bandwidth 3 db coupler.

Directional filters

If a branch line type of directional coupler is made in which the branch line only propagates over a limited frequency range, then the directional coupler will be highly frequency sensitive and may be used to separate, or combine, signals of different frequencies.

A simple form of such a device consists of a cavity coupling two waveguides. Over the narrow bandwidth of the cavity the device acts as a directional coupler but outside the passband the two waveguides are virtually isolated. Similar arrangements may be made using TEM lines where the coupling element is a half wave section. Fig. 6.12(b) shows arrangements for one type of directional filter.

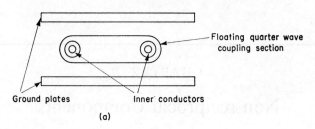

(a)

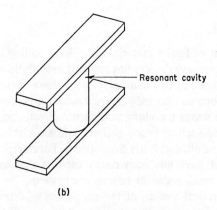

(b)

Figure 6.12.

(*a*) Co-axial coupler.

(*b*) Simple directional filter. **The resonant cavity couples the two cavities via coupling holes in the waveguide walls.**

CHAPTER 7

Non-reciprocal Components

Ferrite devices

The development of ferrite materials that have sufficiently low loss to be used in microwave devices has resulted in a whole new range of components. There are two main classes of these devices, the non-reciprocal components that may be used where it is required to distinguish between waves travelling in different directions, and various reciprocal devices such as phase shifters and switches that may be electronically controlled at fairly high speeds. Parametric devices are also possible but have not been much used as they compare unfavourably with semiconductor parametric systems.

Detailed theoretical studies of the properties of ferrite materials have been made, but are quite involved. Furthermore the insertion of ferrite materials, with their complex magnetic properties, into a microwave component can result in field configurations that are extremely difficult to calculate and as a result a good deal of the design of ferrite components is carried out by experimental methods. In this chapter a highly simplified treatment of the properties of ferrites is given and this will enable the reader to appreciate some of the ideas underlying the design of these components.

Permeability of magnetized ferrites

The most important magnetic effects in solids are due to the natural spins of electrons about their own axis within the atoms of the materials. The application of an external magnetic field causes these electron spins, which constitute magnetic dipoles, to try and align themselves with the applied field. In the case of paramagnetic materials the atoms, and hence the spinning electrons, are far enough apart not to influence each other but in ferromagnetic substances the electron spins are close enough to reinforce each other's effect and the resulting magnetic effect is very much stronger. The ferromagnetic materials thus have fairly large magnetic permeabilities. Unfortunately, they also tend to have fairly high conductivities and if a high frequency magnetic field is applied quite large eddy currents flow, with resultant power loss.

Another class of materials are the ferrimagnetic ones. These materials have two separate crystal lattices and, although the electron spins in each lattice influence their neighbours and hence give a strong magnetic effect, the alignment of the spins in the two lattices is in opposite directions with respect to the applied field. However the resulting magnetizations of each individual lattice are not equal and there is a net magnetic effect. The great advantage of some of the ferrimagnetic materials is that they have a fairly low conductivity and hence at high frequencies the eddy currents are greatly reduced. The general formula for the ferrite materials is $MeO \cdot Fe_2O_3$ where Me is a divalent metal ion. Natural ferrite is Fe_2O_3 but modern ferrite materials are synthetic. Another useful range of ferrimagnetic materials are the garnets. These are so called because of their resemblance to natural garnet but are manufactured rare-earth materials having the general formula $5Fe_2O_3 \cdot 3Me_2O_3$, where Me is a rare-earth metal ion.

The ferrite materials combine fairly high permeability with very low conductivity. They also have a low dielectric loss and a relative permittivity of a few tens.

Permeability of magnetized ferrites

At microwave frequencies the effect that is of the greatest importance in the ferrite materials is spin resonance. This is a complex phenomenon and the following simple picture of the mechanism involved is a gross simplification. For most microwave purposes the ferrite is magnetized to saturation by an applied magnetic field so that its relative permeability is virtually unity if one ignores spin resonance effects. These effects arise as follows. The electron is a spinning charged mass and when the axis of rotation is aligned with an applied magnetic field, as it is in a magnetically saturated ferrite material, it may be likened to a mechanical gyroscope. The force equivalent to gravity in the case of a true mechanical gyroscope is the force exerted by the magnetic field on the dipole, created by the spinning electron. The situation is shown in Fig. 7.1. If the spinning electron is disturbed from its normal rest position (axis of spin parallel to the field) then it will precess in the manner shown just as a mechanical gyroscope will. The natural precessional frequency can be found from quite simple electro-mechanical considerations. If the angular

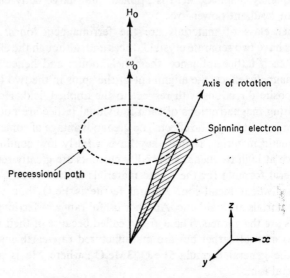

Figure 7.1. Precessional motion of spinning electron.

momentum of the spinning electron is p and its magnetic moment μ_e then the ratio of the two is called the gyromagnetic ratio given by

$$\gamma = -\frac{\mu_e}{p} \qquad (7.1)$$

If the 'applied' magnetic field is H then the natural precession frequency is

$$\omega_0 = \gamma H \qquad (7.2)$$

Here the 'applied' field is that actually affecting the spinning electron. Due to internal fields in the material it will not be equal to the externally applied field.

Suppose that the applied field contains both d.c. and a.c. components so that

$$H = H_0 + he^{j\omega t} \qquad (7.3)$$

For the special case where $\omega = \omega_0$, if there are any components of field in the x or y direction (see Fig. 7.1) then the natural precessional rotation will be synchronous with the applied field and the rotation will build up steadily. Energy is transferred from the r.f. field to the stored mechanical energy associated with the precession. In the absence of any loss mechanism this amplitude of precession would increase continuously but various loss mechanisms limit the process and a steady amplitude of precession is eventually reached. The additional stored energy in the system, caused by the r.f. magnetic field, must represent an increase in the permeability of the material. Furthermore this increase only occurs when the applied angular frequency of the magnetic field is equal to, or near, ω_0. It will also be noted that this effect does not occur if the a.c. field only has components in the z direction. Thus the permeability due to spin resonance is a tensor quantity, i.e. a function of direction.

In the foregoing it is assumed that the material is magnetically saturated. This is necessary both to ensure that the electron spins are all aligned with the applied d.c. field and that the relative permeability in the absence of the a.c. field is nearly unity so that the hysteresis losses are very small. Eddy current losses are, of course, small due to the low conductivity of the material.

If the simple treatment of the spinning electron in the applied field is developed (Appendix 1) for the case of an applied r.f. field of the form

$$h = ih_x + jh_y + kh_z \qquad (7.4)$$

then the r.f. magnetizations in the x, y and z directions are given by

$$m_x = \frac{\gamma M_0}{\omega_0{}^2 - \omega^2}(\omega_0 h_x - j\omega h_y) \qquad (7.5)$$

$$m_y = \frac{\gamma M_0}{\omega_0{}^2 - \omega^2}(j\omega h_x + \omega_0 h_y) \qquad (7.6)$$

$$m_z = 0 \qquad (7.7)$$

where M_0 is the saturation magnetization, ω the frequency of the a.c. component of applied field, and ω_0 is the natural precessional frequency determined by $\omega_0 = \gamma H$. We have chosen H_0 to lie along the z axis and as the material is saturated the magnetization M_0 also lies along this axis.

The r.f. magnetization can then be related to the applied field by the susceptibility tensor, χ,

$$m = \chi.h \qquad (7.8)$$

G

where χ is given by

$$\chi = \begin{bmatrix} \chi_x & \chi_y & 0 \\ \chi_{yx} & \chi_{yy} & 0 \\ 0 & 0 & 0 \end{bmatrix} \quad (7.9)$$

and where

$$\chi_x = \chi_{yy} = \frac{\omega_0 \omega_M}{\omega_0^2 + \omega^2} \quad (7.10)$$

$$\chi_{yx} = \chi_{xy} = \frac{j\omega\omega_M}{\omega_0^2 - \omega^2} \quad (7.11)$$

$$\omega_M = 4\pi\gamma M_0 \quad (7.12)$$

The above expression gives the susceptibility and uses gaussian units as these are commonly used in the study of magnetic materials. However when electromagnetic waves in ferrites are studied it is more convenient to work in terms of the permeability. Obviously the permeability will be a tensor quantity also, and it will be given by

$$\boldsymbol{\mu} = \mu_0 \begin{bmatrix} \mu - & j\kappa & 0 \\ -j\kappa & \mu & 0 \\ 0 & 0 & 1 \end{bmatrix} \quad (7.13)$$

where

$$\mu = 1 + \chi_x \quad (7.14)$$

$$j\kappa = -\chi_{xy} \quad (7.15)$$

Again gaussian units have been used here for the magnetic properties of the ferrite material. It is more convenient to use MKS units when considering electromagnetic wave problems and the quantities μ and κ then become

$$\mu = 1 + \frac{\gamma^2 H_0 \dfrac{M_0}{\mu_0}}{\gamma^2 H_0^2 - \omega^2} \quad (7.16)$$

$$\kappa = \frac{\omega\gamma \dfrac{M_0}{\mu_0}}{\gamma^2 H_0^2 - \omega^2} \quad (7.17)$$

The tensor permeability can be used in the normal Maxwell equations for the solution of problems involving ferrites in microwave devices. However, the tensor permeability of the ferrite, together with the fact that permittivity differs considerably from air, makes many practical systems very difficult to analyse.

So far we have only considered the very simple problem of the effect of spin resonance on one spinning electron. In a ferrimagnetic material the overall effect of all the spins on the various lattices is extremely involved but the resultant effect is similar to that obtained from considering one electron, namely a tensor permeability that changes very rapidly as the frequency of the applied r.f. field is varied around the gyromagnetic resonance value. It will be seen from (7.16) and (7.17) that the permeability can be positive or negative, the negative values being obtained when $\omega > \omega_0$.

Damping

So far we have not considered any loss mechanisms in the spin resonance process, although we have mentioned that they prevent the precessional movement building up indefinitely. The losses are mainly due to spin waves produced by the spin resonance and are a maximum when the applied r.f. frequency equals the gyromagnetic resonant frequency. Either side of this frequency the losses fall off fairly rapidly. If it is required to use the tensor permeability properties of the ferrite, then, to avoid undue loss, it must be operated away from resonance. In certain cases the loss mechanism can be utilized, as it is in a resonance isolator. It is convenient to represent these losses by considering the susceptibility tensor, and hence the permeability tensor, to be complex, e.g.

$$\chi_{xx} = \chi_{xx}' - j\chi_{xx}'' \qquad (7.18)$$

$$\chi_{xy} = -\chi_{xy}'' - j\chi_{xy}' \qquad (7.19)$$

From these we obtain the permeability factors μ and κ for the permeability tensor as

$$\mu = \mu' - j\mu'' \text{ where } \mu' = 1 + \chi_{xx}', \mu'' = \chi_{xx}'' \qquad (7.20)$$

$$\kappa = \kappa' - j\kappa'' \text{ where } \kappa' = \chi_{xy}', \kappa'' = \chi_{xy}'' \qquad (7.21)$$

The variation of the real and imaginary parts of susceptibility with the applied field is shown in Fig. 7.2(a). It will be seen that the real part of the susceptibility is negative below gyromagnetic resonance and positive above whilst the imaginary part, which represents the loss component, follows a curve rather similar to a Q curve.

In practice one is often interested in the variation of the susceptibility with the frequency of the applied r.f. for a constant d.c. magnetic field. These curves are shown in Fig. 7.2(b).

Effect of electromagnetic waves on magnetized ferrites

In general the permeability of a magnetized ferrite sample is complex

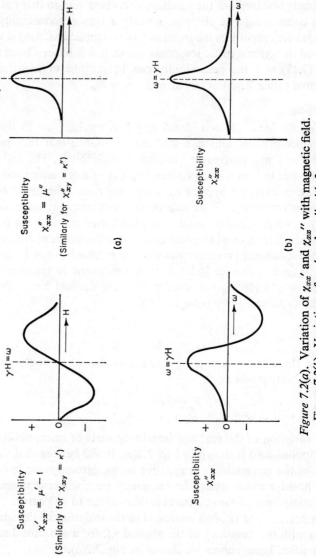

Figure 7.2(a). Variation of χ_{xx}' and χ_{xx}'' with magnetic field.

Figure 7.2(b). Variation of χ_{xx}' and χ_{xx}'' with frequency.

(a)

Susceptibility
$\chi_{xx}'' = \mu''$

(Similarly for $\chi_{xy}'' = \kappa'$)

$\gamma H = \omega$

Susceptibility
$\chi_{xx}' = \mu' - 1$

(Similarly for $\chi_{xy}' = \kappa'$)

$\gamma H = \omega$

(b)

Susceptibility
χ_{xx}''

$\omega = \gamma H$

Susceptibility
χ_{xx}'

$\omega = \gamma H$

and varies rapidly when the frequency of the applied r.f. field is near the gyromagnetic resonance frequency, provided that the r.f. field contains components perpendicular to the applied d.c. field. By varying the applied field the permeability of the material, and hence the transmission properties of the wave passing through the ferrite, can be varied considerably and various devices such as phase shifters and switches can be made.

A special case to consider is that where the applied wave has field components in the x and y direction (assuming the d.c. field to be in the z direction) that are in time and phase quadrature. In this case the resultant magnetic field vector is rotating. This rotating field vector will only cause spin resonance to occur if it is in the same

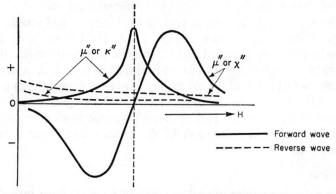

Figure 7.3. Complex susceptibility for a wave travelling in the forward and reverse directions in a magnetized ferrite specimen.

direction as the natural direction of spin precession. Under these circumstances the complex susceptibility varies in the manner shown in Fig. 7.3. If, however, the direction of rotation is in the opposite sense then no spin resonance occurs and the properties of the ferrite are that it has a relative permeability near unity and a small loss. In the case of a travelling wave with a circularly rotating magnetic field component the direction of rotation depends upon the direction of travel of the wave. Reversing the direction reverses the sense of rotation of the magnetic field. Thus spin resonance may occur for a wave travelling in one direction through the ferrite but not for waves travelling in the other direction. This important non-reciprocal property is widely used and the complex permeability for circularly polarized waves travelling in either direction is shown in Fig. 7.3.

Ferrite devices may be divided into two main classes. Firstly there are reciprocal devices in which the effect of the ferrite is the same for waves travelling in either of two directions. This type of device can only be made by arranging that there is no rotating component of magnetic field in the x–y plane. Secondly there are devices which are non-reciprocal and which are made by ensuring that there is a rotating component of magnetic field. Provided that the device is operated somewhere near the spin resonance condition the properties of the ferrite vary greatly for waves in opposite directions.

In both the reciprocal and the non-reciprocal devices it is possible to operate either near spin resonance, where the material is lossy, or far enough away from resonance for the loss to be small but the effective permeability considerably different from unity.

The width of the resonance peak in both the real and imaginary parts of the curves shown in Figs. 7.2 and 7.3 depends on the material employed provided that the internal field in the material is constant throughout its volume. In practice this is seldom achieved and the actual width of the curves is greater than the minimum possible due to variations in the magnetic field strengths within the volume of the material. This variation may sometimes be exaggerated deliberately in order to make the device operate over a wide bandwidth.

Isolators

An isolator is a non-reciprocal two port device that allows power to flow in one direction with a very small insertion loss but has a very large insertion loss for waves travelling in the opposite direction. The isolator is usually adjusted so that in the reverse direction it presents a matched load to the reverse wave and absorbs virtually all the reverse power within itself. In the forward direction it is arranged to appear as a low loss section of transmission line. The scattering matrix of an *ideal* isolator is thus

$$S = e^{j\theta} \begin{vmatrix} 0 & 0 \\ 1 & 0 \end{vmatrix}$$

where θ is the phase shift in the forward direction. In practice there is a small forward loss, which can be as small as 0·1 db, and a very small transmission in the reverse direction, representing a loss of around 30 db for reverse transmission.

The two main classes of isolators are field displacement types and resonance isolators.

Resonance isolators

It is seen from Fig. 7.3 that if the magnetic field applied to the ferrite is adjusted so that the gyromagnetic resonant frequency equals that of the applied field, then, if the applied wave has a rotating component of magnetic field in the x–y plane that rotates in the direction of the natural spin precession, power is absorbed as the material is quite lossy. If the direction of the wave is reversed then the direction of rotation of the magnetic field vector is also reversed and the ferrite then appears to the reverse wave as a low loss material having a relative permeability of almost unity. Thus if the reasonable interaction between the ferrite and the wave can be achieved one wave will be almost completely absorbed whilst the other is completely transmitted.

Examination of Fig. 7.3 would indicate that the imaginary part of the permeability, that is the loss component, is only reasonably large over a fairly small range of field values for a given frequency or, conversely, a fairly small range of frequencies for a fixed magnetic field value. However, even if the externally applied magnetic field is quite uniform the internal fields in the magnetized specimen will vary considerably and so the range of frequencies over which the ferrite appears quite lossy for waves in one direction may be quite large. Furthermore the applied external field may be made deliberately non-uniform to increase the spread of frequencies for which there is loss and broad band isolators may be made. If it is required to measure the true resonance properties of ferrite materials it is necessary to use extremely small specimens in order to ensure that the field within the specimen is reasonably uniform.

Examples of resonance isolators for waveguide, stripline and co-axial cable are shown in Fig. 7.4. The magnetic field configuration for the TE_{10} waveguide was shown in Fig. 1.6. Remembering that the field pattern is moving down the waveguide at the phase velocity, it is apparent that, with the exception of the longitudinal plane lying along the centre of the broad face of the waveguide, there exists naturally a rotating component of magnetic field. Thus a piece of magnetized ferrite placed asymmetrically in the guide will experience a rotating magnetic field and with a suitable value of applied d.c. field resonance will occur for one direction of propagation with consequent loss. The loss in this direction, and the other as well, is obviously related to the length of the ferrite sample used and thus the ratio of the forward to the reverse loss is determined by the ferrite length. A compromise has to be reached between the two losses in a practical isolator and typical isolators have a forward loss of 0·3 db and a reverse loss of 35 db.

In stripline and co-axial cables a TEM mode exists and there is no naturally rotating component of magnetic field. However by distorting the normal field pattern and making it asymmetrical a field

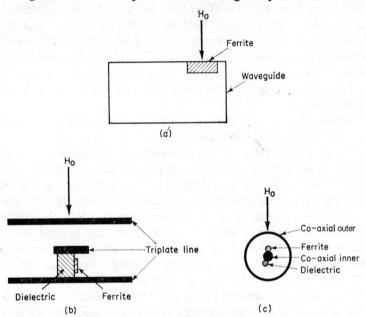

Figure 7.4. Resonance isolators.

(a) Waveguide.

(b) Stripline.

(c) Co-axial cable.

with rotating magnetic components can be produced. The usual method of achieving this is to place a piece of low loss dielectric material, having a relative permeability of about 10 to 20, in the line as shown.

The ferrite is placed close to the dielectric slab as the circularly rotating magnetic field components are strongest at this point. Typical arrangements for co-axial line and stripline are shown in the diagrams. It is often found convenient to construct the isolator in stripline even if a co-axial cable system is being used as transitions from stripline to co-axial cable can be fairly easily made at each end. Discontinuities produced by the ferrite and the dielectric may be reduced by tapering or stepping the shape of the material at each end.

Some frequency characteristics of typical isolators are shown in Fig. 7.5 and it is seen that broad band operation is possible.

The resonance isolator is able to dissipate reasonably large powers, as the ferrite slab in which the power is dissipated is in contact with the metal walls of the transmission line or guide. In the waveguide

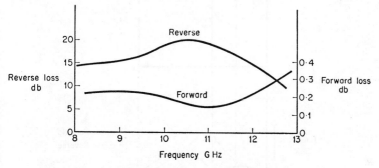

Figure 7.5. Performance of wide-band isolator.

and stripline types it is in contact with the outside wall and water cooling may be used by placing water pipes on the outside of the guide or line. Peak powers of several MW and mean powers of several hundred KW (though not with the high peak powers quoted) may be handled by modern isolators. There are two high power limitations. Firstly a rise in temperature causes changes in the properties in the magnetized ferrite which result in a deterioration of its performance. Secondly the application of a very high field strength in itself causes changes in the properties. Thus cooling of the ferrite is not a complete solution to the problem of operating at high powers.

Field displacement isolators

In this type of isolator the ferrite is operated off resonance so that the losses are small but the permeability of the magnetized ferrite varies very considerably for forward and backward waves. A waveguide field displacement isolator is shown in Fig. 7.6. The normal field patterns of the waveguide are distorted because the permittivity of the ferrite is considerably greater than that of air. In addition to this dielectric disturbance the permeability of the ferrite further distorts the field pattern, and does so in a non-reciprocal manner. The system is arranged so that electric field patterns for the forward and backward directions of propagation are as shown on the diagram. By mounting a piece of resistive card at the point shown, at

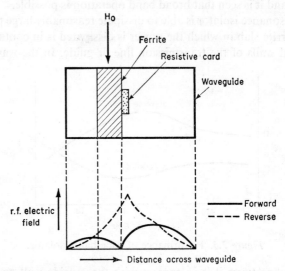

Figure 7.6. Field displacement waveguide isolator. The lower diagram shows the electric field distribution across the waveguide for forward and reverse directions of propagation.

which the electric field is zero for the forward wave, a non-reciprocal attenuation is obtained.

The advantage of this type of isolator is that very low forward attenuations can be obtained. The disadvantage lies in the low powers that can be dissipated in the resistive card, usually less than a watt.

Faraday rotation

Consider a circular waveguide supporting a TE_{11} mode filled, or partly filled, with a piece of ferrite magnetized along the axis of the waveguide. A plane polarized wave has a magnetic field vector in a given direction and this vector may be considered as two equal counter-rotating vectors, i.e. two circularly polarized waves. If the ferrite is magnetized so as to be somewhere in the spin resonance region, then one of these two counter-rotating vectors will be travelling through a medium that has a relative permeability of about unity whilst the other one, that is, the one rotating in the same direction as the natural precession, will experience a very different permeability. In a reciprocal medium both vector components experience the same permeability and rotate, with distance, equal and opposite amounts as they travel down the guide, thus preserving the plane of polarization. However, if one component rotates more than the other, as will be the case with magnetized ferrite, then the resultant vector and the plane of polarization will rotate also. This effect, known as Faraday rotation, is a well-known phenomenon at optical frequencies, and at radio frequencies in the ionosphere which has a tensor permittivity.

Faraday rotation isolator

This device is illustrated in Fig. 7.7. The Faraday rotation section is arranged to change the plane of polarization by 45°. It is seen that the physical arrangement is such that the electric field of the forward wave is perpendicular to the plane of the resistive card but that of the

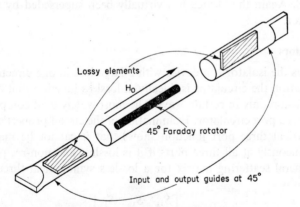

Figure 7.7. Faraday rotation isolator.

reverse waves is parallel to it. The backward wave is thus absorbed with little attenuation of the forward wave.

This type of isolator has largely been superseded by other more simple types. However it has certain advantages at very high frequencies over resonance isolators as it is not necessary to have the ferrite operated at resonance, thus the very high magnetic field needed for millimetre wave resonance isolators is avoided.

Faraday rotation circulator

By omitting the resistive card and arranging various other ports

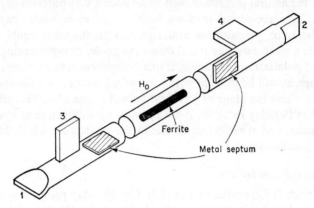

Figure 7.8. Faraday rotation circulator.

Faraday rotation may be utilized for a circulator as shown in Fig. 7.8. Again this device has virtually been superseded by the Y circulator.

Circulators

Whereas the isolator is a device with a large loss in one direction of propagation the circulator is, ideally, a lossless junction that allows transmission only in certain ways. The most widely used component is the three port circulator. Examination of the circuit properties of a symmetrical three port junction shows that it cannot be matched simultaneously at all three ports if it is lossless and non-reciprocal. The general scattering matrix for a lossless symmetrical three port junction is

$$[S] = \begin{bmatrix} S_{11} & S_{12} & S_{13} \\ S_{21} & S_{22} & S_{23} \\ S_{31} & S_{32} & S_{33} \end{bmatrix}$$

The unitary properties plus the necessity of a match at each port result in only two possible matrices (see Chapter 3, p. 51).

The first possible matrix is

$$[S] = \begin{bmatrix} 0 & 0 & 1 \\ 1 & 0 & 0 \\ 0 & 1 & 0 \end{bmatrix}$$

which is the scattering matrix for a perfect circulator with a counter-clockwise sense of direction as shown in Fig. 7.9. Insertion of the alternative condition gives a circulator with the opposite sense of direction.

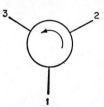

Figure 7.9. Direction of power flow in circulator.

The field displacement three port Y circulator

In this type of circulator a symmetrical 120° Y junction is made in stripline or waveguide. In the centre of the junction is placed, in the case of the waveguide version, a post mode of ferrite, and in the stripline version two discs of ferrite as shown in Fig. 7.10(*a*). The ferrite is magnetized as shown. The complete field solution of this type of device is rather involved but may be found in the references given. A physical picture of the method of operation can best be gained by considering the stripline version of the circulator. In the absence of any magnetizing field, the application of a signal to port 1 will produce a field pattern as shown in Fig. 7.10(*b*). Ports 2 and 3 will be excited by fields that are 180° out of phase with those at port 1 and will have equal outputs. The pattern is produced by two counter-rotating field patterns of identical configuration. The application of a magnetic field to the ferrite results in differing permeabilities for the two modes, dependent upon their direction of rotation with respect to the spinning electrons in the ferrite, and the resulting combined field pattern is no longer symmetrical but has a zero at port 3 and a maximum which is near, but not quite opposite, port 2, as in Fig. 7.10(*c*). By careful design of the transitions between the three strip-line arms and the centre part of the junction, very good matches can be obtained so that virtually all the input power appears at port 2, port 3 being isolated. Reversing the magnetic field reverses the direction of circulation of the power. Stripline circulators can be made in the UHF region as well as the microwave region and circulators are available to 100 MHz. By using stripline, the size and weight of the circulator can be kept down even at these comparatively low frequencies.

At X-band and above, waveguide three port circulators become quite compact and are widely used. Extremely low insertion losses, down to 0·06 db, can be obtained.

An interesting new development is the microstrip circulator. Here a 120° Y junction is made in microstrip and a small ferrite disc is

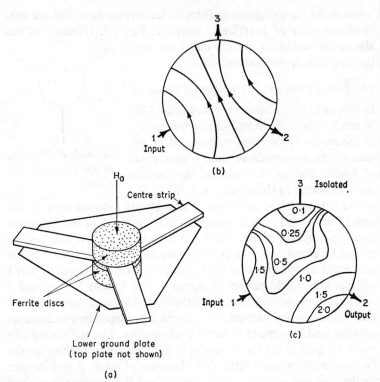

Figure 7.10(a). Stripline Y circulator. The three striplines are usually terminated in co-axial connectors. An abrupt stripline to co-axial connection can be made with a good v.s.w.r.

Figure 7.10(b) Magnetic field pattern in three port Y junction with ferrite unmagnetized. Power fed into port 1 divides equally, but in antiphase, to ports 2 and 3.

Figure 7.10(c). Magnetic field pattern in three port Y junction with ferrite magnetized. Relative magnitudes of the field strengths are shown on the contours. If power is fed into port 1, then port 3 is isolated, but there is output at port 2. The field maximum is slightly displaced from port 2.

placed in a hole in the dielectric. The result is an ultra-miniature circulator integrated in the microstrip circuit.

Four and five port circulators may be made using similar techniques. The three port Y circulator may be used as an isolator by simply terminating one port in a matched load. The advantages of this type of isolator over other types are that all the power is dissipated in the load, which is external to the ferrite device, and that the overall performance is often better than that of the other forms of isolator.

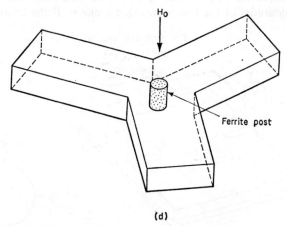

(d)

Figure 7.10(d). Waveguide circulator using three port H plane Y junction.

Some idea of the side range of circulators available and their performance is given below.

Three Port Co-axial Circulators

Frequency range	Bandwidth	Typical properties
140 MHz–20 GHz	10%	20 db isolation, 0·3 db insertion loss
400 MHz–2 GHz	20%	
1 GHz–2 GHz	Octave	18 db isolation, 0·5 db insertion loss

Four and five port circulators are available also. Lumped constant circulators may be made for frequencies down to 30 MHz.

Three Port Waveguide Circulators

Frequency range	Bandwidth	Typical properties
3 GHz–80 GHz	10–15%	20–25 db isolation, 0·2 to 1·0 db insertion loss

Special circulators for communication systems may be made with losses as low as 0·05 db.

Differential phase shift isolators

If there are two possible transmission paths connecting any two ports of a junction the output at any port depends on the relative phases and magnitudes of the two waves that excite it. If the transmission

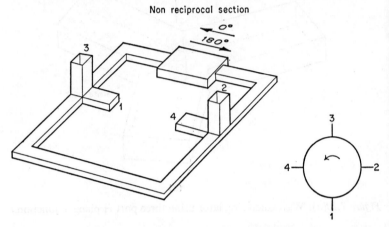

Figure 7.11. Four port circulator using non-reciprocal 180° phase shift section.

path contains a magnetized ferrite sample, then the phase shifts can be non-reciprocal, and hence the performance of the whole junction may be non-reciprocal. A possible arrangement is shown in Fig. 7.11 but numerous other configurations can be used.

Ferrite phase shifters, switches and limiters

In addition to the wide range of isolators and circulators that can be made using magnetized ferrites it is possible to make other devices also.

For instance if the resonance isolator illustrated in Fig. 7.4 is operated away from resonance it becomes a non-reciprocal phase shifter and the phase shift can be varied by altering the applied field. If a reciprocal phase shifter is required then the specimen can be magnetized longitudinally so that the only rotating component of r.f. magnetic field is along the same axis as the d.c. field.

A recent development is the stepped phase shifter. Here the control field is applied by a loop of wire threaded through the ferrite as in a computer's ferrite store. The ferrite is switched to either extreme of its rather square hysteresis loop by current through the wire. The ferrite is placed in a waveguide to give a stepped phase shift and a number of elements may be used to give a wide range of phase shifts.

Microwave switches can be made in a number of ways. One of the simplest is to use a three port isolator in which the direction of the field can be reversed.

Microwave power limiters can be made by using a property of magnetized ferrites that has not yet been discussed. The loss mechanism due to spin waves has already been mentioned but it is found that at high power levels this loss suddenly increases very rapidly with the applied r.f. field strength. This phenomenon can be used to make a microwave limiter.

Low frequency ferrite devices

Most of the devices described so far require a magnetic field that produces a gyromagnetic resonance that is in the region of the operating frequency. In addition the same value of field must saturate the material and it is obvious that at the lower end of the microwave spectrum it is difficult to find materials that have a sufficiently low saturation magnetization. By careful design it is possible to make resonance isolators that will operate down to about 100 MHz. At such frequencies it is often convenient to produce the rotating field by means of striplines that are arranged to cross at right angles and whose path lengths are such that the two waves are in time quadrature at the intersection.

CHAPTER 8

Cavity Resonators and Filters

Cavity resonators

Any cavity will act as a resonator at some radio frequency. That is, if a radio frequency signal is fed into the cavity by a transmission line, it will be found that at some frequency there will be a maximum in absorption of power by the cavity and if a detector is coupled to the cavity there will be a maximum in output from the detector. As the frequency is varied a number of frequencies may be found at which the detector output reaches a maximum showing that the cavity may have a number of different resonant frequencies.

Whilst any shape of cavity may act as a resonator there are some specific shapes which are particularly useful as microwave components. These cavities are derived from sections of waveguide short circuited at both ends. They have resonant frequencies which may be calculated from the dimensions of the cavity and have Q factors which may be determined. An example of this type of cavity formed from a section of TE_{10} rectangular waveguide is shown in Fig. 8.1. The section of guide is terminated at either end by a short circuit plate and the signal and detector are coupled into the cavity in this example by loops fed by co-axial lines. The resonant frequency of the cavity is that at which the length of the cavity is half a guide wavelength or some multiple of this value. When the cavity has this length a standing wave pattern is set up in the cavity. The coupling of the transmission lines to the cavity will affect the resonant frequency slightly because of the reactance coupled to the cavity. In this type of cavity the waveguide mode in the cavity describes the transverse field pattern, in this case the TE_{10} mode pattern. There may be a number of half wavelengths, n, in the field pattern along the cavity and this type of cavity would be described as a TE_{10n} rectangular cavity. (It is possible to have also a TE_{10n} circular cavity.) The simplest form of this cavity is the TE_{101} cavity in which the cavity is one half wavelength long. When waveguide transmission lines are used it is convenient to couple the guide to the cavity by coupling holes. If the resonant frequency of the cavity is to be varied the electrical length of the cavity must be varied. This may be done by making one of the end plates of the cavity movable inside the waveguide forming the cavity. This involves having sliding contacts at the point where the end plate touches the side wall or alternatively a choke plunger may be used. This type of short circuit plunger is illustrated in Fig. 5.1. Small variations in the resonant frequency

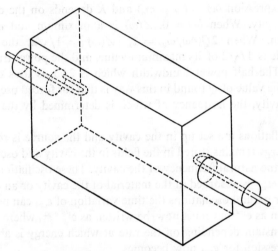

Figure 8.1. Rectangular waveguide cavity with loop coupling.

may be obtained by using tuning screws which protrude into the cavity and the length of which is variable. These screws introduce added reactance into the cavity. It may not be possible to use screws at high power levels as the breakdown level in the cavity will be reduced in the vicinity of the screw. The difficulty due to contact at the plunger may be eliminated by using a type of cavity in which there is no current flow between the side wall and the end wall of the cavity. The field pattern in the TE_{10n} circular cavity is of this type and this form of cavity is often used in measurements as the Q of the cavity is not affected by poor contacts. However as the TE_{10} circular mode is not the dominant mode a cavity of this type with a given dimension may resonate in other modes.

Q Factor of cavity resonators

If a constant level signal is fed into a cavity and the output measured a resonance curve is produced. The output signal is related to the input by the transfer impedance of the cavity, $Z(\omega)$, a function of frequency. If e_{out} is the output voltage for an input current i_{in}

$$e_{\text{out}} = i_{\text{in}}Z(\omega) \tag{8.1}$$

For a high Q cavity near resonance

$$Z(\omega) \simeq \frac{K}{1 + j2Q(\delta\omega/\omega_0)} \tag{8.2}$$

In this expression $\delta\omega = (\omega - \omega_0)$ and K depends on the coupling to the cavity. When $\delta\omega = 0$, $Z(\omega)$ is a maximum and e_{out} is a maximum. When $2Q(\delta\omega/\omega_0) = 1$, $|Z(\omega)| = 1/\sqrt{2}$, the output amplitude is $1/\sqrt{2}$ of its maximum value, and the power transfer is halved. The half power bandwidth which is $2\delta\omega$, is thus equal to ω_0/Q. The value of Q found in this way is that for forced oscillations in the cavity, the frequency of which is determined by the outside source.

If oscillations are set up in the cavity and the source is removed, some energy remains stored in the fields in the cavity and oscillations occur at the natural frequency of the cavity. These oscillations decay as the energy is absorbed in the material of the cavity or an external load. For natural oscillations the time variation of e_{out} can no longer be written as $e^{j\omega t}$ but must now be written as $e^{j(\omega + j\alpha)t}$ where α is the decay constant depending on the rate at which energy is absorbed. The expression for e_{out} now becomes

$$e_{\text{out}} = i_{\text{in}}.Z(\omega + j\alpha) \tag{8.3}$$

but as there is no input $i_{\text{in}} = 0$ and e_{out} is only finite when $Z = \infty$ or

$$\frac{1}{Z(\omega + j\alpha)} = 0 \tag{8.4}$$

If there are no losses $\alpha = 0$ and $\omega = \omega_0$, the unloaded resonant frequency. The losses produce some detuning and the frequency of oscillation is complex, $\omega = \omega_0 + j\alpha$. This frequency may be compared with that for forced oscillations $\omega = \omega_0 + \delta\omega$. For forced oscillations

$$\frac{1}{Z(\omega)} = \frac{1 + j2Q(\delta\omega/\omega_0)}{K} \tag{8.5}$$

The equivalent expression for natural oscillations is

$$\frac{1}{Z(\omega + j\alpha)} = \frac{1 + j2Q(j\alpha/\omega_0)}{K} \tag{8.6}$$

As e_{out} is finite although there is no input current the transfer admittance is zero for natural oscillations and so

$$1 - \frac{2Q\alpha}{\omega_0} = 0 \tag{8.7}$$

The decay factor α is given by

$$\alpha = \frac{\omega_0}{2Q} \tag{8.8}$$

The value of α depends on the rate of decay of energy in the cavity. If U_0 is the initial stored energy

$$\begin{aligned} U &= U_0 e^{-\alpha t} \\ &= U_0 e^{-\omega_0 t/Q} \end{aligned} \tag{8.9}$$

The energy decays as $e^{-2\alpha t}$ as it depends on the square of the field amplitude.

After one cycle or a time $t = 2\pi/\omega_0$ the stored energy is $U = U_0 e^{-2\pi/Q}$ and the energy lost in the cycle is

$$\begin{aligned} U &= U_0[1 - e^{-2\pi/Q}] \\ &\simeq 2\pi U_0/Q \end{aligned} \tag{8.10}$$

This expression gives another definition for Q,

$$Q = 2\pi \frac{\text{energy stored}}{\text{energy lost/cycle}} \tag{8.11}$$

The energy lost may be dissipated in the walls of the cavity, in the dielectric filling, or by coupling to external circuits. The overall Q may be written in terms of the Q of the cavity due to each loss alone

$$\frac{1}{Q} = \frac{1}{Q_c} + \frac{1}{Q_d} + \frac{1}{Q_m} \tag{8.12}$$

where Q_c would be the Q of a perfect cavity coupled to the external circuit, Q_d a perfect cavity with a lossy dielectric filling and Q_m the Q of the cavity with loss in the material of the walls but not in the dielectric.

Microwave filters

In microwave systems filters are required for the separation of signals lying within different bands and for the rejection or suppression of unwanted signals. The filters required may be low-pass, high-pass, band-pass or band-stop filters and it may be necessary to construct them in stripline, co-axial line or hollow pipe waveguide form. The filters may take a variety of physical forms depending on the type of waveguide frequency and power level. Whatever the physical construction, however, the usual design method is first to synthesize a lumped constant network with the required transmission properties and then to transform this network to a form suitable for construction as a microwave circuit.

The theory of network synthesis is a subject with an extensive literature. A brief outline of one method of synthesis is given to illustrate the possibilities of synthesizing a network for a given response [1].

Filter design theory

When designing microwave filters, one is usually concerned with a doubly terminated network, Fig. 8.2, with equal terminating impedances, i.e. the filter is to be inserted into an otherwise matched

Figure 8.2. Doubly terminated filter.

system. A filter synthesis process which can be adopted in this case is that due to Darlington. The properties of the filter may be characterized by its scattering matrix. If the power across the load in the absence of the filter is P_{02} and with the filter is P_2, then assuming unity terminating impedances, the insertion loss power ratio is

$$\frac{P_{02}}{P_2} = \frac{1}{|S_{21}(j\omega)|^2} \tag{8.13}$$

and the loss function A is

$$A = 10 \log_2 \frac{P_{02}}{P_2}$$
$$= -10 \log |S_{21}(j\omega)|^2 \text{ decibels.} \tag{8.14}$$

This loss function specifies to transmission properties of the network and is equivalent to specifying the amplitude squared transmission coefficient $|S_{21}(j\omega)|^2$. For a loss-free two-port network

$$|S_{11}(j\omega)|^2 = 1 - |S_{21}(j\omega)|^2 \qquad (8.15)$$

and from this the complex frequency scattering coefficient can be found through the expression

$$S_{11}(s)S_{11}(-s) = 1 - |S_{21}(j\omega)|^2 \qquad (8.16)$$

From $S_{11}(s)$ the input driving point impedance of the filter can be found from

$$S_{11} = \frac{Z_1 - R_0}{Z_1 + R_0} \qquad (8.17)$$

This gives that

$$Z_1(s) = R_0 \cdot \frac{1 + S_{11}(s)}{1 - S_{11}(s)} \qquad (8.18)$$

Thus, on defining a required insertion loss characteristic, the input impedance of the terminated filter can be found. Knowing the input impedance, the network of the filter can be synthesized.

As a simple example, suppose the filter is to be a low-pass filter with a maximally flat amplitude response. Then

$$|S_{21}(j\omega)|^2 = \frac{1}{1 + \omega^{2n}} \qquad (8.19)$$

where ω is the frequency normalized with respect to the cut-off frequency.

For a third order filter $n = 3$ and

$$|S_{21}(j\omega)|^2 = \frac{1}{1 + \omega^6} \qquad (8.20)$$

From this

$$|S_{11}(j\omega)|^2 = 1 - \frac{1}{1 + \omega^6}$$

$$= \frac{\omega^6}{1 + \omega^6} \qquad (8.21)$$

On putting $s = j\omega$

$$S_{11}(s)S_{11}(-s) = \frac{-s^6}{1 - s^6} \qquad (8.22)$$

and $\quad S_{11}(s)S_{11}(-s) = \dfrac{s^3(-s^3)}{(1 + 2s + 2s^2 + s^3)(1 - 2s + 2s^2 - s^3)}$

so that
$$S_{11}(s) = \frac{s^3}{1 + 2s + 2s^2 + s^3} \qquad (8.23)$$

Knowing $S_{11}(s)$, $Z_1(s)$ can be found with $R_0 = 1$ from
$$Z_1(s) = \frac{1 + S_{11}(s)}{1 - S_{11}(s)}$$

This gives that
$$Z_1(s) = \frac{2s^2 + 2s + 1}{2s^3 + 2s^2 + 2s + 1} \qquad (8.24)$$

The network with this input impedance may be found using the Cauer continued fraction method. The resulting network has the

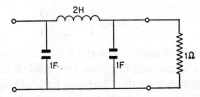

Figure 8.3. A normalized low-pass filter.

form shown in Fig. 8.3. The terminating resistance is provided by the matched system after the filter.

The network required to give other forms of low-pass response may be found using the same method. A transformation of the low-pass filter may be used to give high-pass, band-pass and band-stop filters.

Transformation from low-pass to other forms of filter

(a) High-pass transformation

If ω_0 is the cut-off frequency of the required high-pass filter, the transformation is
$$s = \frac{\omega_0}{s_n} \qquad (8.25)$$

where s_n is the normalized low-pass complex frequency. On writing s in its real and imaginary parts
$$s = \sigma + j\omega = \frac{\omega_0}{\sigma_n + j\omega_n}$$
$$\frac{\omega_0(\sigma_n - j\omega_n)}{\sigma_n^2 + \omega_n^2} \qquad (8.26)$$

When $\sigma_n = 0$

$$\omega = \frac{\omega_0}{\omega_n} \qquad (8.27)$$

The points $\omega = \pm 1$ transform the points $\pm\omega_0$ and points for which $-1 < \omega < +1$ transform to points in the regions $+\omega_0$ to ∞ and $-\infty$ to $-\omega_0$.

(b) Band-pass transformation

In this case

$$s_n = \frac{\omega_0}{\omega_2 - \omega_1}\left(\frac{s}{\omega_0} + \frac{\omega_0}{s}\right) \qquad (8.28)$$

where ω_1 and ω_2 are the band edge frequencies and $\omega_0 = \sqrt{(\omega_1.\omega_2)}$.

(c) Band-stop transformation

In this case

$$s_n = \frac{\omega_2 - \omega_1}{\omega_0\left(\dfrac{s}{\omega_0} + \dfrac{\omega_0}{s}\right)} \qquad (8.29)$$

where ω_0, ω_1, ω_2 are defined as for the band-pass case.

Table 8.1. Filter transformations

LOW-PASS ELEMENT	TRANSFORMS TO		
LOW PASS	HIGH PASS	BAND PASS	BAND STOP
Inductance L_n	Capacitance $C_h = \dfrac{1}{\omega_0 L_n}$	Series resonant circuit $L_{p1} = \dfrac{L_n}{\omega_b}$ $C_{p1} = \dfrac{\omega_b}{\omega_0{}^2 L_n}$	Parallel resonant circuit $L_{s1} = \dfrac{L_n \omega_b}{\omega_0{}^2}$ $C_{s1} = \dfrac{1}{L_n \omega_b}$
Capacitance C_n	Inductance $L_h = \dfrac{1}{\omega_0 C_n}$	Parallel resonant circuit $L_{p2} = \dfrac{\omega_b}{\omega^2{}_0 C_n}$ $C_{p2} = \dfrac{C_n}{\omega_b}$	Series resonant circuit $L_{s2} = \dfrac{1}{C_n \omega_b}$ $C_{s2} = \dfrac{C_n \omega_b}{\omega_0{}^2}$

$$\omega_b = \omega_2 - \omega_1 \qquad \omega_0{}^2 = \omega_1.\omega_2$$

The elementary low-pass filter has elements which are inductive or capacitive. The element changes resulting from the frequency transformations are shown in table 8.1.

Filter components at microwave frequencies

When applying lumped circuit concepts to microwave circuits the type of circuit components which may be constructed must be borne in mind. In microwave circuits resonant cavities may be used in place of the resonant circuits in lumped circuits and reactive obstacles may be used in place of inductors or capacitors. It is also possible to use sections of transmission line as impedance convertors or transformers.

If a section of transmission line of length l is terminated by an impedance Z_R the input impedance is given by

$$Z_m = Z_0\left(\frac{Z_R \cos \beta l + jZ_0 \sin \beta l}{Z_0 \cos \beta l + jZ_R \sin \beta l}\right) \qquad (8.30)$$

If the length of the line is a quarter wavelength, $\beta l = \pi/2$, and

$$Z_{1n} = \frac{Z_0^2}{Z_R} \qquad (8.31)$$

The section of line acts as an impedance invertor changing a load impedance of Z_R to an input admittance of (Z_R/Z_0^2).

If the section of line is approximately half a wavelength long the equivalent circuit is that shown in Fig. 8.4. The reactance of the series arm is $X = Z_0 \sin \phi$ where $\phi \simeq \pi$. This may be written when ϕ is small as

$$X = Z_0(\phi - \pi) \qquad (8.32)$$

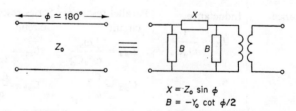

$$X = Z_0 \sin \phi$$
$$B = -Y_0 \cot \phi/2$$

Figure 8.4. Half wavelength section of line and equivalent circuit.

If the guide wavelength at the centre of the band of interest is λ_{g_0} and at an adjacent frequency is λ_g, then $\phi/\pi = \lambda_{g_0}/\lambda_g$ and

$$X = \pi Z_0\left(\frac{\lambda_{g_0}}{\lambda_g} - 1\right) \tag{8.33}$$

An equivalent circuit for this section of line is an inductor and capacitor in series, a series resonant circuit. This has the same form of variation of impedance with frequency as the section of line and the equivalent circuit component values may be found by equating the slopes of the reactance/frequency curve at the resonant frequency. The reactance of the lumped components is

$$X = \omega L - \frac{1}{\omega C} \tag{8.34}$$

At the centre frequency ω_0, $\omega_0{}^2 = 1/LC$ and at this frequency

$$\frac{\mathrm{d}X}{\mathrm{d}\omega} = L + \frac{1}{\omega^2 C} = 2L \tag{8.35}$$

For the transmission line

$$\frac{\mathrm{d}X}{\mathrm{d}\omega} = Z_0\frac{\mathrm{d}\phi}{\mathrm{d}\omega} \simeq \pi Z_0\left(\frac{\dfrac{\lambda_{g_0}}{\lambda_{g_2}} - \dfrac{\lambda_{g_0}}{\lambda_{g_1}}}{\omega_2 - \omega_1}\right) \tag{8.36}$$

The value of the series inductance is therefore

$$L = \frac{\pi Z_0}{2\omega_0 \mathrm{w}}\left(\frac{\lambda_{g_0}}{\lambda_{g_2}} - \frac{\lambda_{g_0}}{\lambda_{g_1}}\right) \tag{8.37}$$

where

$$\mathrm{w} = \left(\frac{\omega_2 - \omega_1}{\omega_0}\right) \quad \text{and} \quad \omega_0 = \left(\frac{\omega_2 + \omega_1}{2}\right)$$

It follows that

$$C = \frac{2\omega}{\pi Z_0\omega_0} \cdot \frac{\lambda_{g_1}\lambda_{g_2}}{\lambda_{g_0}(\lambda_{g_1} - \lambda_{g_2})} \tag{8.38}$$

The microwave lumped reactances and distributed circuit components are used to form filters based on the lumped constant circuits but these circuits must be transformed to a suitable form.

Transformation of the lumped constant circuits

The type of transformation of the basic low-pass circuit which may be used to produce a band-pass circuit is shown in Fig. 8.5(a). The low-pass circuit is first transformed to a circuit with series resonant circuits in series and parallel resonant circuits in shunt. This circuit may then be transformed to a circuit with series resonant circuits coupled by quarter wave impedance inverters, Fig. 8.5(b). The values of L and C in the series arm are provided by a suitable half wavelength section of transmission line. The values depend on the size and type of line and the operating frequency and are fixed for a given line size. The values of L and C provided by the transmission line will not, in general, be those given by the basic band-pass circuit. The basic values of L and C and the impedance of the terminating

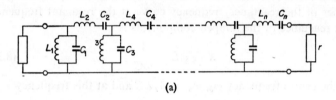

(a)

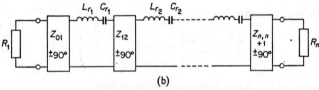

(b)

Figure 8.5. Band-pass filter circuit transformations.

loads must be modified to maintain the same resonant frequency and Q for the resonator as is required in the basic circuit. The equivalent circuits in this transformation are shown in Fig. 8.6. The values of inductance and capacitance in the basic circuit are L_2, C_2, L_3, C_3. If the values of the inductances and the terminating impedances are multiplied by a factor Lr_2/L_2 and the values of the capacitances by L_2/Lr_2 then the resonant frequency and the Q of the circuits is held constant. After bringing the values of the series arm to the required level the shunt arm is converted to a series arm using a quarter wave transformer. The impedance of the transformer line is found by equating the two values of Y_3 in Fig. 8.6(b) and (c). This gives

$$\mathrm{j}\left(\omega C_3 - \frac{1}{\omega L_3}\right)\frac{L_2}{L_{r2}} + Y_4 = \frac{1}{Z^2_{23}}\left\{\mathrm{j}\left(\omega L_{r3} - \frac{1}{\omega C_{r3}}\right) + Z^1_4\right\} \quad (8.39)$$

or $$Z_{23} = \sqrt{\left(\frac{L_{r2}L_{r3}}{L_2 C_2}\right)}, \quad L_{r2}C_{r2} = L_2 C_2 = \frac{1}{\omega_0{}^2} \quad (8.40)$$

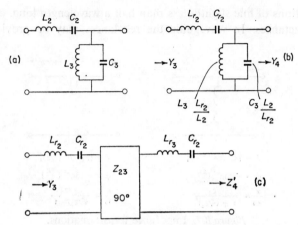

Figure 8.6. Shunt-series transformation.

In general the impedance required or the invertor between sections k and $k + 1$ is

$$Z_{k,k+1} = \frac{\omega_0 \text{w}}{\omega_1^1} \sqrt{\left(\frac{L_{rk} L_{r,k+1}}{g_k g_{k+1}}\right)}, \quad L_k C_{rrk} = \frac{1}{\omega_0^2} \quad (8.41)$$

where $\text{w} = (\omega_2 - \omega_1)/\omega_0$, $\omega_0 = \sqrt{(\omega_1 \omega_2)}$, and ω_1^1 is the pass band edge of the basic low-pass circuit. The impedances of the input and output sections are

$$Z_{01} = \sqrt{\left(\frac{L_{r1} R_1}{C_1}\right)} = \sqrt{\left(\frac{\omega_0 \text{w}}{\omega_1^1} \cdot \frac{L_{r1} R_1}{g_1}\right)} \quad (8.42)$$

and

$$Z_{n,n+1} = \sqrt{\left(\frac{\omega_0 \text{w}}{\omega_1^1} \cdot \frac{L_{rn} R_n r}{g_n}\right)} \quad (8.43)$$

The impedance inverting section may be provided by a section of line of the required characteristic impedance $Z_{k,k+1}$ a quarter of a wavelength long. It is often more convenient to use a section of line containing shunt inductance or series capacitance, Fig. 8.7. These sections of line have an effective characteristic impedance which depends on both the line impedance and the reactance in the line and the reactance introduces a negative electrical length of line. In a transmission line circuit the negative electrical length may be taken into account by reducing the length of the lines on either side of the reactance. In filter sections when the half-wave resonators are coupled by these reactive sections the length of the half-wave resonators is reduced. The transmission line filter then becomes a number of sections of line slightly less than half a wavelength long, coupled by reactances. In waveguide the reactances may be provided by

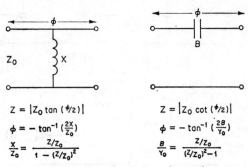

$$Z = |Z_0 \tan (\phi/2)|$$
$$\phi = - \tan^{-1} \left(\frac{2X}{Z_0} \right)$$
$$\frac{X}{Z_0} = \frac{Z/Z_0}{1 - (Z/Z_0)^2}$$

$$Z = |Z_0 \cot (\phi/2)|$$
$$\phi = - \tan^{-1} \left(\frac{2B}{Y_0} \right)$$
$$\frac{B}{Y_0} = \frac{Z/Z_0}{(Z/Z_0)^2 - 1}$$

Figure 8.7. Impedance transformations.

inductive irises or posts. In co-axial or stripline series capacitance may be used by putting suitable gaps in the conductors.

Practical forms of filter

The type of band-pass filter described here finds wide use in microwave circuits although when built with inductive irises or posts the power handling capacity of the system may be reduced. When high-pass filters are required it may be convenient to use wideband band-pass filters with the required lower cut-off frequency as these may be designed and constructed accurately.

Band-stop filters

In some microwave circuits band-stop filters are required to suppress the transmission of unwanted frequencies. This type of filter is required for example in high power transmitters for the suppression of spurious frequencies produced in the transmitter, and in receivers for the suppression of harmonic frequencies produced in mixer circuits.

The lumped constant circuit of a band-stop filter is shown in Fig. 8.8(*a*). This has parallel resonant circuits, in series, and series resonant circuits in shunt. This circuit may be transformed into those shown in Fig. 8.8(*b, c*) using the same methods as were used for transforming the band-pass filter circuits. The form with series reactance may be used with stripline or co-axial line circuits whilst that with shunt reactance is more suited to waveguide circuits. In the first case capacitively coupled short circuited lengths of line may be

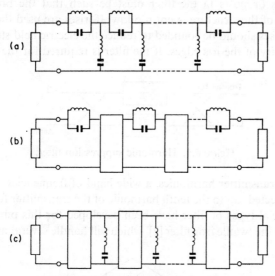

Figure 8.8. Band-pass filter circuits.

used as series resonant circuits whilst in the second case cavities coupled to the waveguide by inductive slots may be used. In waveguide the coupled cavities may have to be spaced threequarters of a wavelength apart because of the size of the cavities. As in the case of the band-pass filters the detailed calculation of the component sizes required is treated in the literature [2].

High power filters

High power transmitters may require filters for the suppression of unwanted frequencies and also for combining the outputs of transmitters working on different frequencies. The transmitter output powers may be several megawatts peak in the case of radar transmitters and in this case the peak powers at the spurious frequencies may be measured in kilowatts.

In the types of filter considered so far there are no dissipative elements and the energy at the unwanted frequencies is reflected back from the filter. In the case of a high power system this reflected power should be absorbed in a dissipative load rather than being allowed to return to the transmitter. If reflective filters are used, this may be achieved by using an arrangement of directional couplers and filters as shown in Fig. 8.9. If reflective filters are used the design of the irises or posts in the filter must be such that the breakdown strength of the structure is not too low. If irises are used the corners of the irises should be rounded to reduce the electric field strength in the vicinity of the iris edges. If the filter is required for the suppres-

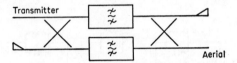

Figure 8.9. Harmonic suppression filter.

sion of transmitter harmonics, a wide band of frequencies may have to be rejected, up to the tenth harmonic of the transmitter frequency, and special types of filter have been developed for this purpose, for example the 'waffle iron filter [2]' which will handle several megawatts

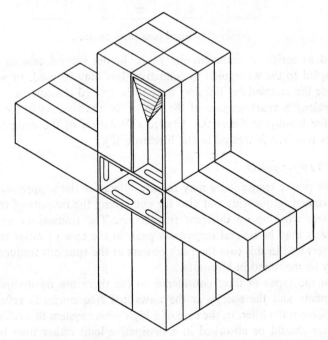

Figure 8.10. High power dissipative filter.

of power and give an attenuation of more than 50 db. over a 10 : 1 frequency band.

To avoid the use of directional couplers to divert the spurious energy, dissipative filters may be used in which the unwanted energy is absorbed in the filter itself. These filters may be constructed by coupling to the main waveguide secondary guides of smaller dimensions which will only support the higher harmonic frequency waves. These secondary guides are loaded with dissipative material to attenuate the unwanted energy. Such an arrangement is illustrated in Fig. 8.10. The secondary guides are coupled by slots in the waveguide wall to the main waveguide. The efficiency of coupling of the harmonic energy to the secondary guides depends on the positioning of the slots and the mode distribution of the harmonic energy in the main waveguide. To allow for different possible modes in the main waveguide the secondary guides may be arranged with several different patterns of coupling slot positions in one filter. Although the filters shown here are in waveguide, similar types of dissipative filter may be constructed in co-axial line.

Tunable microwave filters

Tunable filters are required in some microwave systems, for example to provide radio frequency selectivity in receivers. Such filters may be mechanically tuned or may use the resonance properties of ferrite materials which depend on the applied magnetic field. Mechanically tuned filters may use one or more resonant cavities in waveguide or co-axial line, the physical size of the cavities being controlled mechanically to adjust the passband.

To produce filters the resonant frequency of which may be controlled electrically, the ferrimagnetic resonance properties of some single crystal ferrite materials may be used. Some of the materials which may be used are, yttrium-iron-garnet (YIG), gallium substituted yttrium-iron-garnet (GaYIG), lithium ferrite and barium ferrite. Of these the YIG material has been most used. If a sphere from a single crystal of this material is placed in a steady magnetic field with the crystal axis properly aligned relative to the magnetic field, when a linearly polarized r.f. field is applied at the ferrimagnetic frequency, a circularly polarized r.f. field is set up around the sphere. This field is only excited if the applied field is close to the ferrimagnetic resonance frequency. The effective Q of this resonance may be several thousand, giving a highly selective device which when used in

I

a suitable microwave circuit may be used as a narrow band tunable filter. One method of mounting the sphere is shown in Fig. 8.11.

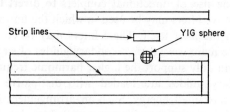

Figure 8.11. YIG tunable filter.

Here the YIG sphere acts as a coupling element between two striplines. Energy is only coupled from one line to the other when the circularly polarized r.f. fields are set up in the coupling hole, that is at the resonance frequency of the sphere.

References

[1] F. F. Kuo, *Network Analysis and Synthesis*, John Wiley and Sons, 1962.
[2] G. L. Mathaei, L. Young and E. M. T. Jones, *Microwave filters, impedance matching networks, and coupling structures*, McGraw-Hill Book Co., 1964.

CHAPTER 9

Joints and Switches

Rotary joints

In some microwave systems it is necessary that movement of one section of transmission line around another can take place. This requirement is often met in radar systems in which the aerial system has to rotate relative to the transmitter and receiver. A small amount of movement is possible if different parts of the system are linked by flexible waveguide. However if continuous rotation is required some kind of rotary joint is needed.

The design of rotary joints is governed by mechanical as well as electrical requirements. The speed of rotation at which the joint must operate, and the elimination of rubbing contacts and surfaces will affect the mechanical design. Electrically, there should be little reflection at the joint and the reflection coefficient should be independent of angle. The joint, particularly in radar systems, may have to operate at high peak power levels. Because the joint must rotate the section of guide in which the angular motion occurs will have to support a circularly symmetrical mode and joints have most commonly been made using co-axial lines or circular waveguides.

Basic co-axial rotary joint

Since the dominant mode in a co-axial line, the TEM mode, is symmetrical about the axis of the line, a rotary joint can be made simply by rotating part of the line about its axis. The simplest form of co-axial rotary joint uses rubbing contacts in the inner and outer conductors. Provided that the rubbing contacts are well designed, this type of joint is satisfactory when the speed of rotation is low, the peak power is low, and electrical noise is not important. It is most useful when extreme bandwidth is required. The joint may be electrically noisy due to the variations in contact resistance. To maintain a good electrical contact, the rubbing contacts may have to be spring loaded, complicating the mechanical design.

The rubbing contacts are usually made of precious metal. One contact may be made of coin silver and the other of carbon impregnated with pure silver. This type of rubbing contact combines good electrical continuity with resistance to wear. It is also self lubricating.

The disadvantages of the rubbing contact type of joint can be

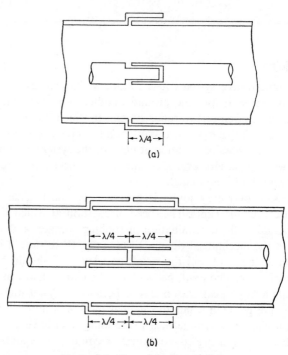

Figure 9.1. Co-axial rotary joints.

(*a*) With quarter wavelength choke sections.

(*b*) With half wavelength choke sections.

overcome by the type of joint using capacity or choke coupling. A choke section is placed in series with the gap between the fixed and rotating parts of the joint so that a low impedance appears at the gap at the microwave frequency.

A simple form of this joint is shown in Fig. 9.1(*a*). The choke section used in both inner and outer conductors consists of a quarter-wavelength section of line terminated in an open circuit. At the joint the open circuit is transformed into a short circuit. Electrical continuity is maintained at the gap under ideal conditions but if dirt collects in the transformer section the impedance at the gap will no longer be a short circuit. Reflection will occur at the gap setting up a standing wave on the main transmission line.

The choke coupling may be improved as shown in Fig. 9.1(b). In both the inner and outer conductors the choke section now consists of a half-wavelength section of co-axial line terminated in a short circuit. This short circuit transforms to a short circuit at the end of the section. Halfway down the section there is a minimum in current flow in the walls of the line and the conductors may be cut at this point to allow rotation without disturbing the electrical conditions. Dirt in the gap now has little effect and a bearing can be inserted without disturbing the electrical performance.

Because this type of design uses sections of line either a quarter or a half-wavelength long, the design is frequency sensitive. The bandwidth over which the joint can be used depends on the v.s.w.r. that can be tolerated on the transmission line and on the particular design of the joint [1].

Basic waveguide rotary joint

The most commonly used form of waveguide in microwave systems had a reactangular cross-section. Since this section is not symmetrical about the axis of the guide, a rotary joint cannot be formed directly in a rectangular waveguide. Instead, a section of co-axial line or circular waveguide must be inserted in which to form the rotary joint.

The first problem, therefore, in the design of a rotary joint for a rectangular waveguide is to design an efficient transition between the rectangular guide and the co-axial line or circular guide. Transitions are discussed in Chapter 10, and so the design problems will not be considered here. It should be remembered, however, that the transition does involve a change of mode: from the TE_{10} mode in the rectangular guide to the symmetrical TEM mode in the co-axial line, or the symmetrical TM_{10} mode in the circular guide.

The usual types of transition used between a rectangular waveguide and co-axial line are the 'crossed line' and 'doorknob' types. In these, the co-axial line is perpendicular to the broad face of the rectangular guide, so that the rotary joint is at right angles to the direction of the waveguide run. The actual form of the rotary joint is the same as that described in the previous section, and the only limitation in the design of these joints is that the length of the co-axial line should be great enough to prevent resonances occurring through the proximity of two mode-exciting transitions. In practice, any asymmetrical modes set up by the transitions are rapidly attenuated, and the limitation in the length of the co-axial section does not impose any serious effect on design.

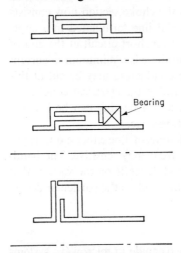

Figure 9.2. Half section diagrams of various forms of waveguide rotary joints.

In the transition between rectangular and circular waveguides, the circular guide must support only the symmetrical TM_{10} mode, and asymmetrical modes such as the TM_{11} mode must be suppressed. The TM_{10} mode can be best excited in the circular waveguide by coupling it into the broad face of the rectangular guide. The circular guide can, in fact, be considered as a cavity fed by the rectangular guide, and since cavities are discussed in Chapter 10, the details of coupling will not be considered further here. In practical joints, further precautions are taken to prevent asymmetrical modes and unwanted resonances being set up by the inclusion of filter rings and suppressors.

The rotary joint in the circular waveguide is similar to that in the outer conductor of a co-axial line. A choke section is inserted in the wall of the guide to place a low impedance in the gap between the fixed and rotating parts of the joint. The choke section uses half-wavelength sections terminated in short circuits, together with quarter-wavelength sections, Fig. 9.2.

Multi-channel rotary joints

In systems where a multi-purpose aerial is used, the range of frequencies to be handled may be too wide for a single-channel rotary joint to transmit. This occurs particularly in airborne equipment where space is limited and the weight of components must be kept to a minimum. In these systems, therefore, the rotary joints used must incorporate more than one channel.

The basic co-axial rotary joint described on page 124 can be adapted to form a multi-channel joint simply by using the outer conductor of one channel as the inner of the next, and so on. The limitation on the number of channels that can be incorporated in this type of joint is determined by mechanical considerations. As only one channel can be used as an 'in-line' joint, the terminations of the other channels must be at right angles to the axis of the joint. Right-angle stub supports must be used to couple co-axial lines to the joint, or wave-guide-to-coaxial-line transitions, which complicate the design of the joint. The dimensions of the conductors have to be chosen so that only the TEM mode is supported in each channel whilst maintaining the characteristic impedance at approximately 50Ω. The choke sections in the conductors of one channel have to be positioned so that they do not interfere with the next channel, and in some channels rubbing contacts have to be used. As a result of these design considerations, although rotary joints containing five channels have been manufactured, the most commonly used joints of this type contain two channels only. The channel-to-channel isolation of a well-designed joint of this type is in excess of 60 dB.

Another type of co-axial rotary joint for multi-channel operation is shown in Fig. 9.3. The joint in the figure is for two-channel operation, and consists of two identical sections. The central conductor is common to both sections, and is fitted with end plates which support the stator probe and matching post for each section. The rotor housing rotates about the central conductor supported by the two bearings, and contains the rotor probe and matching post for each section. The co-axial line formed by the central conductor and the rotor housing supports the TEM mode, and in each section of the joint power is transferred into the joint and extracted from it by the two probes. Radial choke sections are used to produce a low impedance in the gaps between the stationary and rotating parts of the joint, and to isolate the two sections of the joint.

Sections of the two-channel joint can be stacked vertically to form a multi-channel joint. A six-channel joint has been designed [2], the limiting factor being the number of co-axial cables that can be accommodated in the hollow central conductor without affecting the mechanical strength.

Both sections of the two-channel joint shown in Fig. 9.3 are designed to operate over the same frequency band. The channel-to-channel isolation of the two sections is in excess of 40 dB. The two

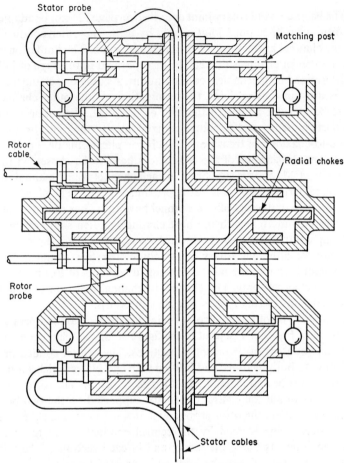

Figure 9.3. Dual rotary joint.
(Reproduced from the *Microwave Journal*, Vol. 17, 1964, p. 71.)

sections can be operated at different frequencies. The central conductor can be stepped to different diameters in the two sections, and the rotor housing, probes, and radial choke sections designed for the particular frequency in the section.

Waveguide rotary joint using directional couplers

A waveguide rotary joint based on principles different from those of the joints previously described has been designed [3]. This joint uses directional couplers, and is shown in Fig. 9.4.

The joint consists of three E plane waveguide rings of the same diameter stacked vertically. Arrays of slots are cut in two coupling diaphragms which are clamped between the upper and middle rings, and the middle and lower rings respectively. These diaphragms act as 0 dB couplers, and provide full power transfer between the upper and lower rings through the middle ring. The middle ring is cut along the electrically neutral axis to allow the upper ring to rotate with respect to the lower ring.

Connections are made to the joint by E plane bends. Matched-load terminations are required for the upper and lower rings, and these can be incorporated inside the rings or fitted outside. As the

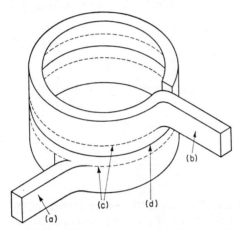

Figure 9.4. Waveguide rotary joint using directional couplers.

directional couplers are more effective the longer they are, it is preferable to fit the terminations outside the joint. They can be coupled by E plane bends similar to the input and output bends.

The operation of the joint depends on the efficiency of the couplers. Resonance effects in the middle ring produce 'stop bands' at particular frequencies at certain angles of rotation of the joint. The number of these frequencies in a particular frequency range depends on the mean diameter of the waveguide rings. This diameter is therefore chosen so that stop frequencies are either outside the frequency range to be transmitted by the joint, or are situated at a point within the band that is not used.

If the joint is required to transmit a 6% bandwidth, the stop frequency can be positioned outside this band. A bandwidth in excess of 10% can be achieved if a 1% stop band is acceptable.

Mechanical switches

Waveguide switches

Simple waveguide switches may be constructed by using a Y junction with a rotatable resonant ring placed in two of the three arms. When either of the rings is transversely across the guide then no power can pass down that guide, whilst, when either ring is placed so that its diameter lies along the longitudinal axis of the guide, very little power is reflected. By means of a suitable mechanism the rings can be rotated through 90°, one ring being in the transverse position whilst the other is in the longitudinal, and vice versa. Thus, power is directed

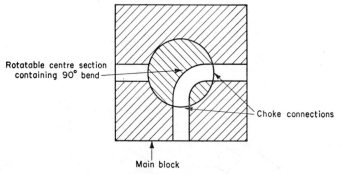

Rotatable centre section
containing 90° bend

Choke connections

Main block

Figure 9.5. Waveguide switch. The centre portion of the block can be rotated so that either pair of ports is connected. The waveguides in the centre and main blocks are connected by choke type flanges (see p. 51) which are not shown in the diagram.

down either of the two output arms of the Y junction. Such simple switches have neither good isolation nor a good SWR and most waveguide switches operate by using a moving section of waveguide as shown in Fig. 9.5. Here a T junction is constructed out of a solid metal block but the centre section of the T is replaced by a cylindrical block containing a 90° bend. This centre section can be rotated so that either of the two output ports can be connected. The centre section is separated from the main block by a small annular gap and a choke coupling is used to make the connection between the main block and the rotable block (see p. 57).

A typical switch of this form, operating up to 18 GHz, has an SWR better than 1·1 and an insertion loss of about 0·2 db. It can be switched at up to 20 cycles per minute. For lower frequencies better

switch performance can be obtained although the speed of switching
is reduced, due to the increased mass of the rotating block.

Waveguide switches are often operated by solenoids but the
switching speed is quite slow, due to the mechanical inertia. For high
speed switching either ferrite devices (see Chapter 7) or semiconductor switches must be used. Another special type of high speed switch
is the TR cell, described in Chapter 10.

Co-axial switches

In co-axial systems the dimensions are such that neither resonant
rings nor choke plungers can be used. Co-axial switches, like their
waveguide counterparts, use moving sections of transmission line but

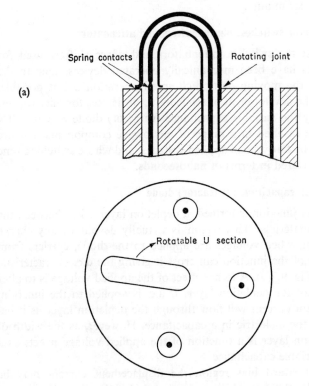

Figure 9.6. Co-axial switch.

(*a*) Cross-section showing rotating U section that connects one common
input port to any of a number of output ports.

(*b*) Plan view of single pole four-way switch.

with spring contact arrangements that enable the moving section to be connected to different fixed sections. Various arrangements are possible and one of them is shown in Fig. 9.6. This is a single pole switch which can have any number of 'ways'. The input co-axial contains a rotary co-axial joint which connects to a rotatable U section of cable. The other end of the U section has spring connections and can be rotated to make contact with any number of output ports.

The v.s.w.r. of co-axial switches can be kept below 1·1 up to about 3 GHz but at higher frequencies the v.s.w.r. deteriorates, being about 1·5 at 12 GHz. Switching speeds for solenoid operated co-axial switches are slightly higher than for waveguide switches, from 50 to 100 cycles per minute.

Semiconductor switches, phase shifters and attenuators

In the past the switches, attenuators and phase shifters used for microwaves have been mechanically operated devices. Due to the inertia of the moving parts high speed operation is not possible. However the development of semiconductor devices for microwaves, particularly the variable capacitance (varactor) diode and the PIN diode have resulted in a range of microwave components that are controlled by fairly small applied voltages, and whose switching time can be measured in terms of nanoseconds.

The variable capacitance (varactor) diode

When a PN junction is formed, a depletion layer arises between the P and N materials. This region is virtually devoid of any charge carriers but, when voltages are applied to the diode, carriers from either side of the junction can cross it giving the d.c. characteristic shown in Fig. 9.7(a). Another effect of the applied voltage is to alter the width of the depletion layer. If a.c. is applied to the junction, displacement current will flow through the depletion layer as it behaves like the dielectric in a capacitance. However, as the width of the depletion layer is a function of the applied voltage it acts as a voltage variable capacitance.

In the forward bias region the displacement current may be swamped by the normal direct current, but if the diode is operated in the reverse bias region, and at reasonably high frequencies, it appears as a reasonably high quality voltage variable capacitor. The capacitance variation is given in Fig. 9.7(b).

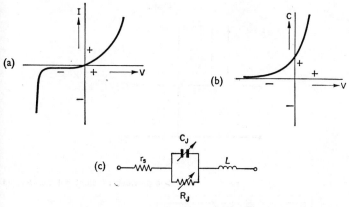

Figure 9.7(a). Current/voltage characteristic of PN junction.
Figure 9.7(b). Capacitance voltage characteristic of PN junction.
Figure 9.7(c). Equivalent circuit of PN junction.

Varactor diode switches

The equivalent circuit of a varactor diode is shown in Fig. 9.7(c). For fairly large reverse bias voltages it appears as a slightly lossy capacitance, whilst, for large forward bias, its impedance is limited by the inductance of the diode mount. In order to obtain maximum isolation and minimum insertion loss the diode is not connected directly to the waveguide or line but is connected via a stub line. The arrangement is shown in Fig. 9.8(a). Normal transmission line consideration leads to the following requirements for the best performance.

$$Z_0' = (L_F/C_R)^{-\frac{1}{2}}$$

$$\tan \theta = \frac{1}{2\pi f_0}(L_F C_R)^{-\frac{1}{2}}$$

(The subscripts F and R denote forward or reverse bias)

The quantities referred to are shown in Fig. 9.8(a) whilst a practical realization of the system is shown in Fig. 9.8(b).

In order that the junction capacitance of the diode should not be so large as to be a virtual short circuit for all bias conditions the junction area, and hence power handling capacity, has to be kept quite small. The power handling capacity of such switches is only a few watts but by using multiple diode arrangements powers of a few tens of watts can be handled. Switching time for varactor switches is usually a few tens of nanoseconds.

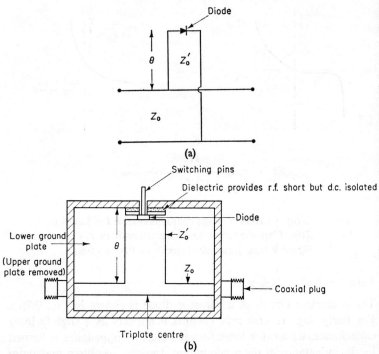

Figure 9.8(*a*). Varactor diode connected to main transmission line via subsidiary line.

Figure 9.8(b). Stripline form of circuit shown in 9.8(*a*).

Varactor diode phase shifters

By keeping the bias in the reverse direction and varying it, the diode impedance remains essentially a capacitive reactance, but varies with the applied voltage. If this variable capacitive reactance is incorporated in the transmission system then it may be used as a phase shifter. As in the case of the varactor diode switch the power handling capacity is limited to a few watts.

PIN diode switches and attenuators

The PIN diode is a PN junction with an intrinsic region sandwiched between the two doped regions (Fig. 9.9(*a*)). At d.c. or low frequencies it operates as a normal diode and, in the forward conducting region, majority carriers from the P and N materials pass across the intrinsic regions and contribute to the normal diode current flow. However, at frequencies in the region of a few tens of kilocycles, the transit time across the intrinsic region is so long compared with the period that carriers do not have time to cross the intrinsic region before the polarity of the applied voltage changes, and they are driven back again. Thus above this frequency the diode appears almost as a linear resistance. However the conductivity of the intrinsic region, normally very low compared with the doped P and N regions, is greatly affected by the injected majority carriers.

If the diode is biased by a d.c. signal and, at the same time, has a

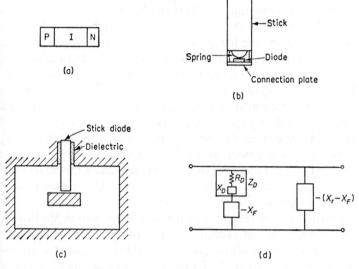

Figure 9.9.

(*a*) PIN diode.
(*b*) Stick diode.
(*c*) Stick diode in stripline.
(*d*) Compensation for diode parameters.

fairly high frequency a.c. signal applied then it appears to the a.c. signal as a linear resistance. However the magnitude of this a.c. resistance depends on the rate of carrier injection into the intrinsic region and this, in turn, is controlled by the d.c. bias. The device appears as a voltage variable resistance. Also, due to the fact that the separation between the P and N regions is long compared with that in a normal PN junction the capacitance of the diode is very small. Typically the capacitance is only 0·2 pf, whilst the d.c. resistance varies from 1 Ω to several thousand ohms when the bias voltage is changed by twenty volts. Because the capacitance per unit area is small compared with varactor diodes, it is possible to use reasonably large junction areas, and the diode can thus handle much more power than the varactor diode.

The PIN diode is commonly mounted on a brass post as shown in Fig. 9.9(b) and this arrangement is known as a 'stick' diode. This enables the diode to be mounted as shown in Fig. 9.9(c). Direct mounting in co-axial or stripline is possible but it is more satisfactory to use a ridged waveguide. The ridge reduces the waveguide impedance to a value of around 30–800 Ω and enables the diode to be connected directly across the guide. The operation of the PIN diode switch is limited by the inductance in series with the diode, and the ridge guide arrangement reduces this series inductance to a minimum.

For operation at X band and above the series reactance due to the inductance of the diode is troublesome and must be tuned out. If the diode can be represented by an impedance $(R_f + jX_f)$ in the forward direction and $(R_r + jX_r)$ in the reverse direction then the forward bias impedance can be reduced to R_f by placing a reactance of $-X_f$ in series with the diode. By placing a further reactance of value $-(X_r - X_f)$ in parallel with the device (Fig. 9.9(d)) the reverse impedance can be made very high also. When this arrangement is placed in a transmission line of known impedance the insertion loss and isolation may be readily evaluated from transmission line theory.

The power handling capacity of the switch can be increased by using a number of diodes suitably spaced along a length of transmission line. A device using 22 PIN diodes can handle a peak power of 30 kW, mean power of 50 W over a frequency range of 1–4 GHz. The switching speed of PIN diodes is around 200 to 500 ns. This should be compared with the speed of 10 ns or so, obtainable with varactor switches.

PIN diode attenuators

By using configurations similar to those used in switches, but by gradual control of the bias, the PIN diode may be used as a microwave attenuator. Again multiple diode arrangements are used to handle reasonably large powers.

It is difficult to obtain a good match with a PIN diode attenuator as the process of altering the attenuation consists of adjusting the value of a lumped parameter in the transmission line and there must be a resultant change in the mismatch. This should be contrasted with waveguide vane attenuators where a distributed lossy element is used, which is tapered so as to give a very small reflection at almost any value of attenuation.

PIN diode limiters and modulators

By using a PIN diode with a short intrinsic region and arranging that the bias provided by the resulting rather imperfect rectification is self-adjusted by the r.f. power, a PIN diode limiter may be used. Whilst the speed of operation is slower than that of the varactor limiter, it can handle higher powers.

Virtually all microwave power sources, when directly modulated, tend to produce a mixture of amplitude and frequency modulation and usually only one of these forms of modulation is required. The frequency spectrum of a microwave oscillator which is intended to be amplitude or frequency modulated usually contains quite large proportions of frequency components which, ideally, should not be present. A more satisfactory arrangement for producing amplitude modulation is to run the microwave source continuously and use a PIN diode attenuator as a modulator. A much cleaner AM spectrum is obtained. In the case of frequency modulation the PIN diode may be used as a limiter to remove any amplitude modulation obtained by directly modulating the microwave source.

Constant amplitude swept frequency sources are finding increasing use for measurements. One difficulty encountered in designing such sources is the large change in output of the backward wave oscillator that occurs when its frequency is electrically changed. This output variation can be partly compensated by grid voltage adjustment. A further improvement can be used by placing a PIN diode attenuator in the output. The d.c. signal to the attenuator is obtained, via an amplifier, from a detector that samples the r.f. power level in the system. By a suitable servo loop the power level can be adjusted by the PIN diode attenuator so that it remains constant within 0·1 db over the whole range of swept frequency. A further advantage of this system is that the power sampling can be performed at any point in the system under test, not necessarily at the oscillator output. This facility to maintain constant power at any point in the system is extremely useful for reflectometer work (see p. 158).

References

[1] G. L. Ragan, *Microwave Transmission Circuits*, *M.I.T. Radiation*
  K

Laboratory Series, Vol. 9, McGraw-Hill Book Co. Inc., New York, 1948, pp. 100–105.

[2] M. Cohen, *A Six-channel Vertically Stacked Co-axial Rotary Joint for the S-, C-, and X-Band Region, Microwave Journal*, Vol. 7, No. 11, Nov. 1964, pp. 71–74.

[3] S. Boronski, *A Multichannel Waveguide Rotating Joint, Microwave Journal*, Vol. 8, No. 6, June 1965, pp. 102–105.

CHAPTER 10

A Few Examples of Microwave Systems

Mixers and modulators

If microwave frequencies are to be used for communication the microwave carrier must be modulated, by some method, with the information that is to be transmitted. After reception of the microwave signal the modulation information has to be recovered.

Various types of modulation are used in different microwave systems. The three main types are amplitude, frequency and pulse modulation. The modulation of the microwave carrier may be carried out either at the microwave oscillator itself or by separate modulating components. Direct modulation of the oscillator is often simple with microwave tubes but the carrier frequency may not be very stable. When a high frequency stability is required from tubes, or if solid state sources are used, it may be easier to modulate the signal separately.

The reflex klystron is frequently used as a microwave oscillator and this type of tube may be readily amplitude or frequency modulated. The amplitude of the carrier may be modulated by control of the grid voltage, the frequency of the carrier may be modulated by control of the reflector voltage. It is simple to frequency modulate klystron valves but more difficult to achieve a linear frequency modulation without amplitude modulation. This is due to the type of mode curve, Fig. 10.1, of the tube. This shows how the amplitude and frequency vary as the reflector voltage varies and it is seen that there is only a small frequency range at the peak of each mode curve at which frequency modulation may be achieved with little amplitude modulation. Special klystrons are available for use in communication systems which have been developed for linear frequency modulation. The reflex klystron may also be pulse modulated although its efficiency is lower than that of the magnetron.

The cavity magnetron is widely used as a pulsed oscillator. The pulse width and repetition frequency are controlled by the supplies to the magnetron. The pulsed magnetron is widely used in radar systems and in some communication systems although its frequency stability is not high. If high frequency stability is required a stable low power source may be used, for example a crystal oscillator followed by a frequency multiplier chain. The output of the frequency multiplier may be modulated in the microwave amplifiers for example by using pulsed klystron or travelling wave tube amplifiers or by frequency modulating the signal in a travelling wave tube by modulation of the helix voltage. If a solid state source is used it is also possible to frequency modulate the first oscillator to give a frequency

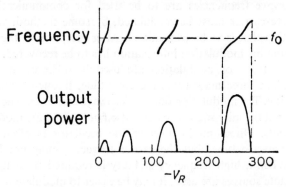

Figure 10.1. Klystron mode diagram.

modulated output, provided that only a small percentage deviation is used.

In some cases it is required that a microwave signal shall be modulated in amplitude after generation and without the use of a separate modulating amplifier. In such a case it may be possible to use ferrite or diode modulators to control the signal. These devices act as current or voltage controlled attenuators. Ferrite modulators use a controlled magnetic field to vary the attenuation of a ferrite loaded section of waveguide. The modulation frequency range is limited by the magnetizing winding inductance, although, by suitable design, pulse lengths of a microsecond or less may be produced. For frequencies above those for which ferrite devices may be used, it may be possible to use diode modulators in which the loss in a diode switch is controlled by the modulating signal.

Microwave mixers generally make use of the non-linear characteristics of silicon diode rectifiers. Generally point contact rectifiers are used. These are available in different mountings for use in the different circuit arrangements which are used in different types of transmission line or waveguide crystal package. Some types are shown in Fig. 10.2. The type of crystal mounting which may be used in waveguide with co-axial crystals is shown in Fig. 10.3. This type of mount is similar to the bar-and-post waveguide to co-axial line

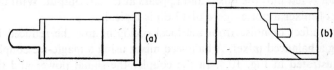

Figure 10.2. Microwave diode packages.

transition but, in the mixer, the bar is insulated from the waveguide and supported by a half-wavelength choke at each end. This choke presents an effective short circuit between the bar and waveguide at

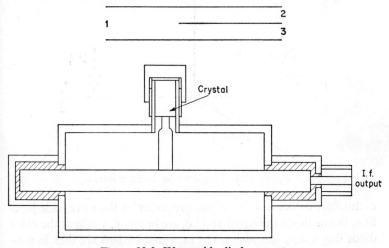

Figure 10.3. Waveguide diode mount.

the waveguide wall for the microwave frequency but not at the intermediate frequency. The intermediate frequency output is taken from the bar through the choke support. The d.c. return must be provided through the i.f. circuit. It is difficult to provide a good match with mixer mounts over a broad band of frequencies and typically a standing wave ratio of 0·6 may be expected.

With this type of mixer both the signal and the local oscillator power must be fed into the waveguide. The local oscillator power is conveniently introduced into the signal guide by using a directional coupler. In a sensitive receiving system detection of signals is limited by noise in the system. Noise will arise in the mixer due to thermal effects and is enhanced by the non-linear mixer characteristic which causes mixing of noise components to give an output at the i.f. In addition with this single diode design, noise on the local oscillator output is fed into the mixer and appears at the i.f. output. With this type of mixer a noise figure of 12 db is typical.

The effect of noise from the local oscillator may be reduced by using a balanced mixer. A balanced mixer using a magic-tee coupler is illustrated in Fig. 10.4. In the coupler the signal power and the local oscillator (l.o.) power are both split, half of each appearing at

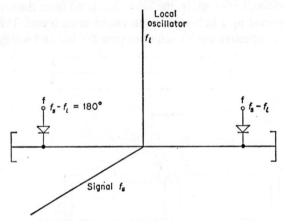

Figure 10.4. Magic tee balanced mixer.

each mixer diode. Because of the properties of the waveguide junction, in one diode the signal and l.o. are in phase, whilst at the other diode they are in anti-phase. The i.f. signal outputs are then in anti-phase, whilst noise components from the l.o. mixing together will appear in phase. By combining the i.f. outputs in a push-pull input to the i.f. amplifier the signal components are added, whilst the noise components tend to cancel each other. With this type of mixer the noise figure of the mixer and i.f. amplifier may be about 8 db. The overall noise figure will depend on the i.f. amplifier noise figure, the local oscillator noise, the balance in the mixer circuits and the type of diode used. A more compact form of balanced mixer can be made using 90° hybrid junctions in co-axial line or stripline. Such balanced mixers will operate over an octave bandwidth or more.

All these mixers accept both r.f. sidebands and signals and noise in both sidebands will contribute to the i.f. output. Filters may be used before the mixer to reduce the response to one sideband, but it is difficult to produce microwave filters that can be tuned rapidly over a band of frequencies. For receivers that are to be tuned over a wide bandwidth, image suppression mixers may be used. The circuit of such a mixer is shown in Fig. 10.5. Two balanced mixers are used. The signal power is fed to the mixers via a magic-tee whilst the

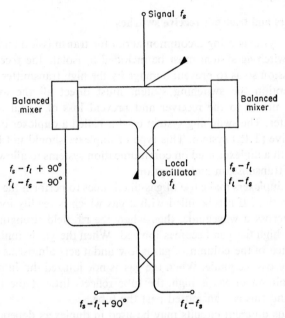

Figure 10.5. Image suppression mixer.

local oscillator power is fed via a 90° hybrid. The signal frequency f_s and the local oscillator frequency f_l appear with different phase relationships on the two mixers as shown in the figure. For the upper sideband the resultant i.f. outputs are $(f_s - f_l)$ and $(f_s - f_l + 90°)$. For the lower sideband the outputs are $(f_l - f_s)$ and $(f_l - f_s - 90°)$. In the i.f. quadrature hybrid the upper sideband frequencies combine at one output port whilst the lower sideband components combine at the second output port. The two sidebands are thus separated and either one or the other can be used.

Another use for mixers is as modulators at medium levels in communication systems. In these systems the baseband signal may be used to frequency modulate an intermediate frequency carrier at say 70 MHz. This f.m. i.f. is fed on to the diode in a mixer. The r.f. carrier is also fed into the mixer where it mixes with the i.f. to give upper and lower sidebands at r.f. The modulated r.f. is reflected from the mixer. A 3 db coupler system may be used to feed the r.f. into the mixer and to extract the modulated r.f. at a second port of the coupler.

Duplexers and transmit-receive switches

In radar systems using a common aerial for transmission and reception a switching system must be included to isolate the receiver on transmission so as to prevent damage by the high transmitter power. On reception the switching system must direct all the available received power to the receiver and prevent loss of signal into the transmitter. The switching system used is called a duplexer or transmit-receive (T.R.) system. This type of duplexer should not be confused with a diplexer used on communication systems to allow simultaneous transmission and reception.

Most duplexers make use of gas-filled tubes to perform the switching operation. If a tube filled with a gas which is readily ionized is placed across a waveguide, then when the r.f. field strength is sufficiently high the gas becomes ionized. When the gas is ionized the impedance of the column of gas is low and it acts almost as a short circuit across the guide. When the gas is not ionized the impedance of the column of gas is high, the tube reflects little of the incident power and this is transmitted past the tube.

Various different circuits may be used in duplexers depending on the power level of the transmitter and the degree of isolation required. These different circuits may be divided into two classes, balanced duplexers and branch duplexers. The circuit of a branched duplexer is shown in Fig. 10.6. The transmitter is connected directly to the main aerial feed line. There are two branches on this feed line spaced approximately a quarter-guide wavelength apart. The branch nearer the aerial feeds through to the receiver. Both branches contain gas-filled cells in cavities. On transmission the high transmitter power ionizes the gas in the cells. The position of the cells relative to the main waveguide is such that when the cells are ionized the short circuit at the cell is transformed to a short circuit at the waveguide

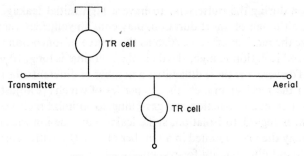

Figure 10.6. Branched duplexer.

wall so that all the transmitter power is fed to the aerial. On reception the gas in the cells is not ionized and power may pass through the receiver branch to the receiver. In the second branch a short circuit is situated beyond the gas cell. By adjusting the position of this short circuit the impedance across the main waveguide at the branch junction can be adjusted to appear as a short circuit. As the distance between the two branches is a quarter-guide wavelength the short circuit across the main guide at the second branch appears as an open circuit at the first or receiver branch, and so all the available received power passes through to the receiver arm. The gas cells are required to have several properties which it is difficult to satisfy together in one cell. The main properties are that the gas should ionize sufficiently quickly to prevent the front edge of the transmitter pulse reaching the receiver, that it should provide a high degree of isolation during the pulse, and that it should de-ionize quickly after the pulse is over. The variation of power passing the cell during the pulse is illustrated in Fig. 10.7. It has been found that cells with good

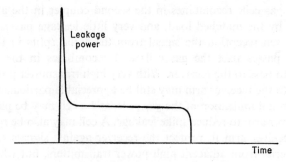

Figure 10.7. Leakage power in a T.R. cell.

isolation during the pulse tend to have a high initial leakage spike which, although of short duration, may contain sufficient energy to damage the receiver crystals. Also as the degree of ionization in cells with good isolation is high, the de-ionization time is long, 10 μsec or more. To overcome these difficulties a number of different cells may be used in the receiver branch, the properties of which are adjusted, by using different construction and gas-filling, to optimize their performance with regard to isolation, spike leakage and de-ionization. The tubes may then be mounted in a number of low Q cavities forming a broad band filter section for reception.

The power handling capacity of a branched duplexer is limited by the isolation provided, the de-ionization time that is allowed, is dependent on the applied power and degree of ionization, and on the breakdown level of the duplexer. To provide a higher power handling capability various types of balanced duplexer have been

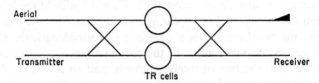

Figure 10.8. Balanced duplexer.

devised. The circuit of one type is shown in Fig. 10.8. This consists of a pair of 3 db directional couplers, separated by a pair of gas-filled cells. Power from the transmitter splits in the first coupler and ionizes both gas cells, which then act as short circuits across the two waveguide sections. The transmitter power is reflected and recombines in the coupler to pass out through the aerial arm. Any power leaking past the gas cells recombines in the second coupler in the arm terminated by the matched load, and very little leakage passes to the receiver. On reception the signal from the aerial splits in the first coupler, passes past the gas cells and recombines in the second coupler to pass to the receiver. With very high transmitter power the leakage to the receiver arm may still be appreciable particularly during the initial ionization of the gas cells, and a cell may be placed in the receiver arm to reduce spike leakage. A cell may also be required in the receiver arm to protect the receiver against signals received by the aerial from adjacent high power transmitters, but which are not of sufficient power to ionize the main gas cells.

Other circuit arrangements may be used to reduce the power level on the gas cells. Two other arrangements are those in Fig. 10.9. In Fig. 10.9(*a*) the balanced duplexer system is modified to include a

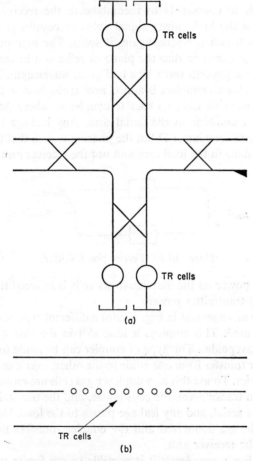

Figure 10.9. High power duplexers.

second pair of couplers and a pair of power sensitive reflecting terminations. The latter consist of a section of waveguide containing a gas cell followed by a short circuit. For low powers the reflecting plane is at the short circuits; for high incident power the gas cell ionizes, shifting the plane of reflection by an amount depending on the position of the gas cell. If the action of the duplexer on reception is considered, first the received signal splits in coupler A and passes to couplers B and C. In each of these couplers the signal splits. If the positions of the short circuits are correct, the signals reflected combine to come out of the fourth arm, so that from both B and C signals pass to coupler D to recombine in the receiver arm. On transmission the high power signal splits in coupler A and passes to couplers B and C where, again, it splits. The high power signal ionizes the gas cells so that the plane of reflection in the two arms containing the gas cells shifts by a half guide wavelength. The signals reflected back into couplers B and C now recombine in the arm on the transmitter side and pass back to coupler A, where their phase is such as to recombine in the aerial arm. Any leakage in couplers B and C passes to coupler D but the phasing is such that the leakage signals combine in the load arm and not the receiver arm. With this

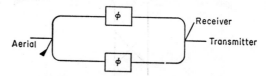

Figure 10.10. Ferrite phase shifter.

system the power on the individual gas cells is reduced to a quarter of the total transmitter power.

With the arrangement in Fig. 10.9(*b*) a different type of directional coupler is used. This employs a long slot in the side walls of the adjacent waveguides. This type of coupler can be made to give complete power transfer from one guide to the other, over a certain range of frequencies. To use this as a duplexer gas cells are mounted across the slot. On transmission the cells ionize, and the transmitter power is fed to the aerial, and any leakage passes to the load. On reception the gas cells are de-ionized and the coupler transfers the received power to the receiver arm.

For the low power levels it is possible to use ferrite switches for receiver protection. These switches may be used in a similar circuit arrangement to the balanced duplexer if the switch acts as a reflecting short circuit when operated. The ferrite device may also be used as a phase shifter in the circuit arrangement of Fig. 10.10. The ferrite devices have a maximum power handling capacity of about 10 kW but as they are controlled separately from the transmitter power the problems of spike leakage do not occur. Also with suitable switch design the recovery time can be small, less than 1 μsec compared with say 10 μsec for a gas switch.

Multichannel communication systems

In microwave communication systems there is a need to use one aerial for a number of transmitters and receivers operating on different frequencies. To separate the different signals various systems of couplers, circulators and filters have been devised. The first circuit example, Fig. 10.11, is that of a simple link providing a single transmitting frequency and a single receiving frequency, on one aerial. In this case the diplexer uses a coupler system of two 3 db couplers, as did the radar duplexer, separated by two filters. The filters accept the received signal frequency but reflect other frequencies. The transmitter which operates at a different frequency to the receiver feeds into coupler A. The power splits and is reflected by the filters. The reflected signals recombine in coupler A to feed out to the aerial. On

Figure 10.11. Diplexer circuit.

reception the wanted signal from the aerial splits in coupler A, passes through the filters and recombines in coupler B to feed the receiver. On reception, unwanted signals are reflected by the filters and recombine in the transmitter arm of coupler A. An isolator may be included in this arm to prevent unwanted signals from entering the transmitter and to isolate the transmitter from reflections of its own power, due to mismatch in the diplexer or aerial system.

The second circuit example, Fig. 10.12(*a*), is that of a multichannel receiver system. In this system a number of different microwave frequencies are received simultaneously, and the signals have to be separated and fed to individual receivers for each frequency. A number of circulators and band-pass filters are used in this example. The whole band of signals enters circulator A by arm 1. The whole band leaves arm 2 and passes to filter A. This filter accepts one frequency from the band, which passes to receiver A. The remaining frequencies are reflected, pass back to arm 2 of the circulator A and leave arm 3 of the circulator. A similar process operates in the following circulators and filters until all the wanted signals have been passed to their respective receivers. Any unwanted signals may be absorbed in the final load to prevent reflection back through the chain of cir-

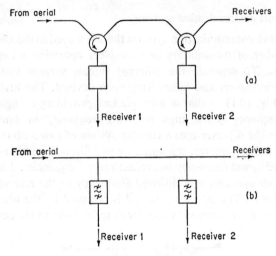

Figure 10.12.

(*a*) Circulator multiplexer.   (*b*) Filter multiplexer.

culators. With this system, employing circulators, the positioning of the filters relative to the circulators is not critical.

A filter system may be used without circulators and using only simple branching circuits to feed the filters, Fig. 10.12(*b*). In this case,

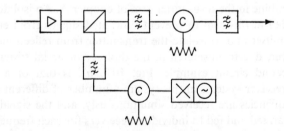

Figure 10.13. High level mixer transmitter.

however, the position of the effective short circuit plane of each filter relative to the main waveguide run is critical and must be adjusted to prevent unwanted reflection at each branch connection.

A type of microwave circuit which may be used in a microwave communication transmitter is shown in Fig. 10.13. The transmitter employs frequency modulation of the r.f. carrier. A 70 MHz f.m. intermediate frequency is mixed with the signal from the microwave oscillator in a high level mixer. From the resultant output, the side-band at the desired microwave frequency is selected by the band-pass filter. This signal may be transmitted directly. In this way a complete solid state transmitter may be built, the output power being dependent on the power of the microwave source. If the power level is too low the signal from the filter may be amplified by a travelling wave tube amplifier. Using a solid state multiplier chain to generate the microwave signal, accurate frequency control is simple, as crystal oscillators may be used to drive the multiplier chain.

Aerial feeder systems

In microwave communication and radar systems feeder transmission lines are needed between the transmitters and the aerial. The type of transmission line used will depend on the frequency, signal band-width and power level. The types of transmission line may be divided into three main classes, co-axial lines operating in the TEM mode,

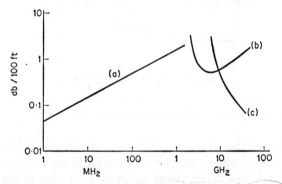

Figure 10.14. Transmission line attenuation.
(a) $\frac{7}{8}$ in diameter air spaced co-axial line.
(b) 2 in × 1 in rectangular waveguide TE_{10} mode.
(c) 2 in diameter circular waveguide TE_{10} mode.

waveguides operating in their fundamental mode, and waveguides operating in higher order modes. The attenuation of some different types of transmission line are shown in Fig. 10.14. This shows how the attenuation of the co-axial line increases with frequency, and that the attenuation of the TM_{10} mode in the rectangular guide has a minimum, whilst the attenuation of the TM_{10} mode in a circular guide decreases with frequency. It must be remembered that the latter mode is not the fundamental mode in a circular guide and care must be taken to preserve the mode and its low loss properties. At high frequencies modes other than the TEM mode may be set up on co-axial lines and again care must be taken to preserve the required mode, and to minimize distortion of the signals being transmitted.

When wideband signals are to be transmitted the disperson in the waveguide may lead to distortion of the signal as different frequency components in the signal will propagate with different velocities. This is illustrated in Fig. 10.15, which shows how the group velocity in a waveguide varies with frequency, relative to the cut-off frequency in the guide. For little dispersion the guide should be operated at a

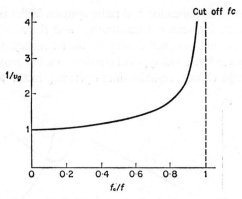

Figure 10.15. Group velocity in a waveguide.

frequency well above the cut-off frequency. Karbowiak [1] has shown how the bandwidth of a waveguide operating in the TM_{10} mode with an amplitude modulated signal varies as a function of the cut-off frequency in the guide and the carrier frequency, Fig. 10.16. The signal bandwidth that may be used also depends on the type of modulation used as some types are more resistant to distortion than other. In particular, p.c.m. may be used when the transmission medium will distort the signal since, with this type of modulation, the signal waveform does not have to be preserved. The only requirement is that the pulses should be detected correctly at the receiver.

Another cause of distortion that may occur in aerial feeder systems is the mismatches, which may cause reflection of the signals within the system. The reflected signals arrive at the receiver with a time delay relative to the main signal. With a wideband signal the delayed component of the signal leads to distortion of the waveform. This

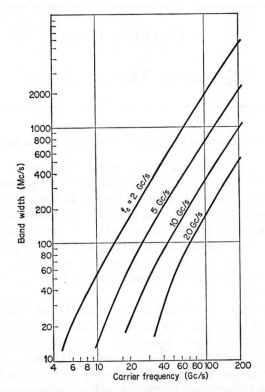

Figure 10.16. Variation of a.m. signal bandwidth with cut-off frequency and carrier frequency in a waveguide supporting TE_{01} circular mode.

(Reproduced by permission from A. E. Karbowiak, *Trunk Waveguide Communication*, Chapman & Hall.)

effect is most important in multi-channel communication systems and leads to inter-modulation distortion in the de-modulated signal channels. For example in a 300 channel telephony system the v.s.w.r. in the system must be less than 1·05 for satisfactory operation.

References

[1] A. E. Karbowiak, *Trunk Waveguide Communication*, Chapman and Hall Ltd, 1965, p. 32.

L

CHAPTER 11

Microwave Measurements

Impedance measurements by measurement of reflection coefficient

In describing the many microwave components in use today, there
has been considerable stress on the need to match the components.
The majority of microwave systems have to be fairly well matched
and in communication systems, where the total distortion over a
large number of links, each containing many components, has to
conform to rigid international standards, an extremely good match
has to be maintained over a broad frequency band. As a result the
measurement of reflection coefficient and impedance is an extremely
important subject.

A very widely used method of measuring the value of an impedance at high frequencies is to use the impedance to terminate a transmission system of known characteristic impedance, and to measure
the reflection produced by this termination. The change produced
in both amplitude and phase of the wave on reflection from the
termination is determined by the ratio of the terminating impedance
to that of the transmission line and the theory has been covered in
Chapter 2. Two basic techniques are available for measuring the
reflected wave. In the first, the spatial standing wave pattern, produced by the reflection, is examined by inserting into the line a small
probe that samples the electric field in the line. By moving the probe
lengthwise along the line for a half-line wavelength the standing wave
pattern can be examined. In Chapter 2 it has been shown that the
important information required is the ratio of the maximum to
minimum value of the electric field and the position of the minima.
In the second method the forward and backward waves are separated
by means of a directional coupler. The separated waves are then
compared to find the reflection coefficient of the terminating
impedance.

Waveguide standing wave indicator

This is usually constructed in rectangular TE_{01} waveguide. As the current flow is entirely longitudinal at the centre of the broad wall of the guide, it is permissible to cut a thin slot at this point to allow the probe to be inserted in the guide. A suitable sliding mechanism enables the probe to be moved along the length of the guide. To prevent the probe itself disturbing the system, its penetration must be very small compared with the waveguide height. As the probe output varies with its penetration into the guide, the sliding mechanism must be very accurately made so that the penetration does not alter as the probe is moved. At very high frequencies, where the waveguide height, and hence the allowable probe penetration, is small, the mechanical accuracy required is quite difficult to achieve, being around 0·0002 inch for a good indicator at 10 GHz and this factor largely accounts for the high cost of this instrument, which is usually called a standing wave indicator.

The sensitivity of the instrument is improved by providing two variable stub lines that can be used to tune the capacitance of the probe. The r.f. voltage from the probe is applied to a semiconductor rectifying diode and the rectified output fed to a suitable indicator. The output is usually quite small but it can be detected with a galvanometer. However it is generally more convenient to amplitude modulate the microwave source at a few kHz so that the diode output then has an audio frequency component. This may then be amplified by a tuned amplifier and applied to a fairly robust indicating instrument.

The general form of a waveguide standing wave indicator is shown in Fig. 11(a). The problems of construction are virtually all mechanical. The waveguide must have a very accurate cross section and the probe penetration must be accurately maintained for all longitudinal positions of the probe.

Co-axial standing wave indicators (slotted lines)

A technique similar to the above may be applied to co-axial systems. The only difference is that the size of co-axial cable normally used is rather small, compared with the size of a waveguide for the same frequency, and for mechanical reasons it is sometimes necessary to make the standing wave indicator (slotted line) in a larger size of line. The larger line is arranged to have the same characteristic impedance as the rest of the system but transition sections have to be used to change the cable size. These sections have to be very carefully designed if they are not in themselves to produce reflections and they

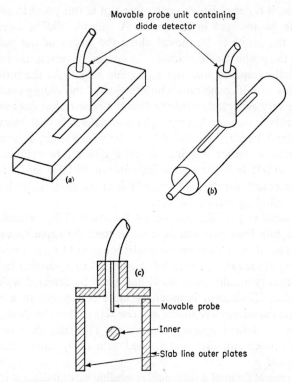

Figure 11.1(a). Waveguide standing wave indicator.
Figure 11.1(b). Co-axial standing wave indicator.
Figure 11.1(c). Slab line standing wave indicator (cross section).

impose a further restriction on the possible accuracy of the instrument. The slotted line section of the instrument is not restricted to the co-axial form and some instruments are made using a slab line (parallel plate line) and a 'non-slotted line' has also been made. Some of these are illustrated in Fig. 11.1(b), (c).

Techniques used in standing wave measurements

1. *Calibration of the instrument.* This is usually achieved by using the instrument to measure a known pattern and that given by short

circuit is generally used. A lossless line terminated in a short circuit
has an electric field that varies longitudinally as $\sin(2\pi z/\lambda_g)$, where z
is the distance measured from the short circuit. The position of the
distance scale on the indicator may be checked by measuring the
distance between two minima to find λ_g and then checking to see that
the minima are λ_g/zz from the short circuit.

The use of a semiconductor diode that has a V/I relationship of
the form

$$I = I_0(e^{ev/kt} - 1) \qquad (11.1)$$

means that the detected current is not directly proportional to the
voltage from the probe. At low levels equation (11.1) gives a virtual
square law relationship but for accurate measurements this must be
checked for the diode used. If the diode output is measured as a
function of distance when the indicator is terminated in a short
circuit, then as the field pattern varies as $\sin(2\pi z/\lambda_g)$ and if the
diode law is taken to be

$$I = kV^n \qquad (11.2)$$

then a plot of $\log I$ versus $\log.\sin(2\pi z/\lambda_g)$ will yield a straight line
whose slope is the diode index, n, which is usually about 2.

2. *Measurement of very small standing wave ratios.* When s is small
the ratio of the maximum to minimum field is large and this ratio is
further exaggerated by the diode law. Thus the lowest reading of the
indicator may be difficult to measure accurately. A more accurate
technique [1] is to note the minimum reading of the indicator, using
a sensitive detector, and then move the probe until k times the
minimum electric field is obtained. The probe is then moved until
the same reading is obtained at a point on the other side of the
minimum position. The distance, w, between the two points at which
k times the minimum field is obtained is related to the standing wave
ratio thus

$$s = \frac{\sin(\pi w/\lambda_g)}{[k^2 - \cos^2(\pi w/\lambda_g)]^{\frac{1}{2}}} \qquad (11.3)$$

Charts are available that enable the normalized width between the
two points, i.e. the actual distance divided by the guide wavelength,
to be converted directly to s.w.r. If the detector is square law and the
probe is moved until twice the minimum detector reading is obtained,
then for small values of s equation (11.3) can be approximated thus

$$s = \pi w/\lambda_g \qquad (11.4)$$

Reflectometers

In this instrument the forward and reflected waves are separated by a directional coupler (see Chapter 6) and the modulus of the reflection coefficient is obtained, directly, by comparing the two. The device may be adjusted, by terminating it in a short circuit and adjusting the gain of the detectors in the two arms, until equal indications are obtained. The s.w.r. that can be measured is limited by

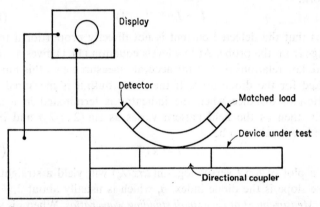

Swept frequency oscillator

Figure 11.2. Reflectometer using swept frequency oscillator.

the directivity of the coupler used. Care must be taken to accurately match the two auxiliary arms of the coupler also.

Phase information cannot be obtained from the simple reflectometer but it is a very useful instrument for swept frequency work as a suitable display system may be arranged which gives the reflection coefficient directly on an oscilloscope as shown in Fig. 11.2.

The time domain reflectometer. In this system a very short pulse is sent down a microwave transmission system, and if there are any discontinuities in the system there will be partial reflection of the pulse. By displaying the reflected pulses on an oscilloscope the magnitude and position of the discontinuities may be found, rather as in a simple rangefinding radar system. The time interval between the transmitted and received pulses is, of course, very small when the transmission system is short, and a normal, simple oscilloscope display would not give sufficient high time resolution. However, the sampling oscilloscope (see p. 177) overcomes this difficulty and makes the system practicable.

Other measurements using reflection measurements

So far we have only considered the measurement of reflection coefficient when the line has been terminated in an unknown impedance,
that is a one port device. Obviously the techniques described may
be used to find the reflection coefficient at any port of a multi-port
device. The terms S_{mm} of the device's scattering matrix are then
known. In the case of two port device further information may be
obtained by using a circuit theorem. This theorem states that if, in
any two port (four terminal) device, the impedance connected to one
port is varied in such a manner that its locus on the complex plane
describes a circle then the impedance locus looking into the other
port also describes a circle. By comparing the two impedance circles
the properties of the two port may be obtained in the form of the
complex scattering matrix.

The coefficients may be obtained from the two circles by a geometrical construction described and proved by Deschamp [2].

In the case of a lossless two port device a complete reflection will be
obtained if the terminating impedance is a short circuit, and the above
principle may be used to obtain the properties of the two port device
quite easily [3]. One port is terminated in a movable short circuit
and the input standing wave pattern is examined using a slotted line.
If both the two port device and the short circuit are lossless then
the s.w.r. is almost zero and only the minimum position need be
measured. The short circuit is then moved in steps through $\lambda_g/2$
and the position of the minimum noted for each position of the short
circuit. A plot of $(2\pi/\lambda_g)(d_1 + d_2)$ is then made versus $(2\pi/\lambda_g)d_1$
where d_1 and d_2 are the distances of the plunger and node, respectively, from some arbitrary plane. The resulting curve will take the
form shown in Fig. 11.3. The peak to peak ripple on this curve is
designated δ_{max} and the standing wave ratio is then given by

$$s = \tan^2\left(\frac{\pi}{4} - \frac{\delta}{2}\right) \tag{11.5}$$

Obviously if there is no ripple the s.w.r. is unity. This method, usually
known as Feenberg's [3] method, is very useful when the s.w.r. is near
unity, that is when the values of maximum and minimum electric
field strength are nearly equal, and normal s.w.r. measurements
based on the ratio of maximum to minimum field are difficult to
make accurately. Frequently the two port device under investigation
is a small discontinuity caused by an imperfect coupling. For many

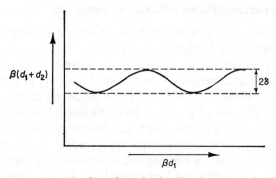

Figure 11.3. Plotting of results for Feenberg's method.

purposes good matching is essential and the small imperfections in the match may be measured by this method.

Measurements at very low power level

It is sometimes necessary to make slotted line measurements in systems where the maximum tolerable power level is very low. As the probe of the slotted line only extracts a very small fraction of the available power, it may be found that the diode output is then not measurable. Under these circumstances the positions of the power source and the detector may be interchanged. This procedure is justified by the reciprocity theorem. Such a technique is very valuable when making measurements on receiver input circuits, tunnel diode or parametric devices, etc.

Impedance bridges, waveguide

In these the unknown impedance is compared with a known standard as in low frequency measurements. A bridge using a magic tee (a hybrid ring could also be used) is shown in Fig. 11.4. Power entering arm 1 splits equally and in phase down arms 2 and 3. If the two terminating impedances in arms 2 and 3 are equal, then the reflected signals add when they return to the junction and pass back along arm 1, and no output is obtained in arm 4. The known impedance can be a short circuiting plunger and a calibrated attenuator. The insertion loss of the attenuator limits the range of measurement. As the wave passes through the attenuator twice, the reflection coefficient amplitude is related to twice the attenuator reading. Calibration of the bridge is achieved using a short circuit in place of

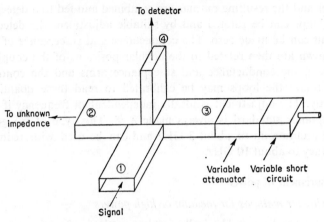

Figure 11.4. Magic tee bridge.

the unknown. (See also Chapter 6 for a more detailed description of the magic tee junction.)

Co-axial impedance bridges

Four co-axial cables are connected to the unknown, a source and a conductance and susceptance standard as shown in Fig. 11.5. Three magnetic coupling loops sample the magnetic field in three of the

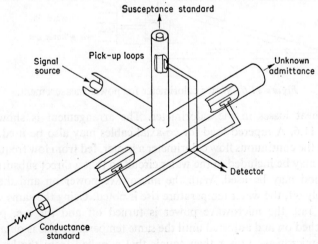

Figure 11.5. Co-axial admittance bridge. Parts of the co-axial outer have been cut away to show the pick-up loops.

cables and the resulting outputs are combined and fed to a detector. The loops can be rotated and by suitable adjustment the detector output can be made zero. The conductance and susceptance of the unknown are then related to the angular positions of the coupling loops in the conductance and susceptance arms and the controls that rotate the loops may be calibrated to read these quantities directly. The adjustment is ideally independent of frequency if the susceptance standard is always made $\lambda_g/8$. This type of bridge is quite accurate up to about 3 GHz and can be used with reduced accuracy to about 10 GHz.

Measurement of power

Calorimeter methods for medium or high powers

One of the earliest, and basically simplest, methods of power measurement is to absorb the microwave power in a load and measure the heat thus produced. A tapered water load mounted in a waveguide can provide a good matched termination and the heat rise in the water, produced by the microwave power, can be measured. For high powers a continuous water flow is used, for low powers the rate of temperature rise is measured. Precautions have to be taken to allow

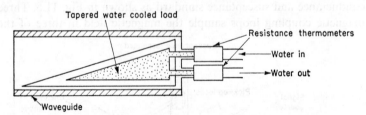

Figure 11.6. Water calorimeter for power measurement.

for heat losses in the calorimeter. The arrangement is shown in Fig. 11.6. A tapered load for co-axial cables may also be used.

In the continuous flow calorimeter a heater, fed from low frequency a.c., may be included in the water circuit so that a direct substitution method may be used. With the microwave power on and the a.c. supply off, the water temperature rise is noted. Using the same water flow rate the microwave power is turned off and the a.c. power switched on and adjusted until the same temperature rise is obtained. The microwave power then equals that supplied from the low frequency a.c. source. This system depends on the water flow rate being held constant and various balanced flow calorimeters are available which avoid this difficulty by using a separate a.c. heated section and simultaneously noting the temperature rise in this section and the microwave load.

Disadvantages of water calorimeters are:

(a) Measurements of powers less than a few watts are difficult.

(b) A constant flow water supply is needed.

(c) All the microwave power is absorbed.

However, for many purposes, such as testing high power tubes, they are quite satisfactory and can dissipate high powers where necessary.

Bolometers and thermistor wattmeters

In these instruments, either all, or part, of the available power is absorbed by a resistive element. The change in temperature due to the absorbed power causes a change in the resistance of the element. The element is connected in a bridge circuit, which may be directly calibrated so that the out of balance bridge current indicates the microwave power, or a self-balancing bridge may be used. Alternatively, a substitution method may be used by switching off the microwave power and applying d.c. power to obtain the same resistance change. The thermistor element consists of a small bead of semi-conducting material suspended between two fine wires and has a very high negative temperature coefficient. With a suitable bridge unit the thermistor may be used to measure powers of a few microwatts at frequencies up to about 40 GHz. The thermal time constant of the thermistor is fairly long and thus it cannot be used to detect sudden changes in power level. However, it can be used to measure the mean value in a pulsed system and its time constant makes it able to stand heavy overloads for a short time. A wide variety of thermistor mounts are available in both co-axial cable and waveguide. In the former, mounts are available in both to equal the cable characteristic impedance and very wide band operation is possible. These devices will stand a large overload as excessive power alters the thermistor resistance so much that it becomes a very poor match and most of the excess power is reflected. In waveguide mounts suitable matching elements are built in to the mount so that a good match is obtained and all the power is absorbed in the thermistor. The bandwidth for accurate measurements is limited by the operating range of the particular waveguide used and the matching arrangement.

A number of commercial thermistor power meters are made with self-balancing bridges. In this type of bridge the power supply is 50 Hz and is variable. As the thermistor is a non-linear element, the values of the bridge arms may be chosen so that with all the elements at ambient temperature the bridge does not balance but with a suitable applied 50 Hz bridge voltage, but no microwave power, the bridge balances due to the change in resistance of the thermistor element, caused by the 50 Hz heating. The balance may be made automatic by using the out of balance bridge voltage to control the 50 Hz supply voltage, via suitable amplifying stages. If microwave power is applied to the bridge then it remains balanced due to the self-balancing arrangement and this has the advantage that the thermistor element always has the same resistance, thus ensuring a good microwave match. Power measurement in the self-balancing bridge is by measuring the voltage across the thermistor element. This can be achieved by using a differential type of meter using a second, or 'slave' bridge.

Self-balancing bridges in conjunction with thermistors can be used to make accurate measurements of powers down to a few microwatts. Very careful stabilization of all the bridge supplies is essential for these low power measurements, but satisfactory instruments are available that will measure powers from a few microwatts to about 10 mW.

Bolometer meters consist of a very thin wire in a suitable waveguide or co-axial mount and have a positive temperature coefficient. The bolometer has a much shorter time constant than the thermistor but will only stand small overloads before burning out. Sudden bursts of power will destroy it. Its sensitivity is similar to that of the thermistor.

Bolometer and thermistor devices are so sensitive that power measurements at levels above about 1 mW may be made without absorbing more than a very small fraction of the total power. A directional coupler is used to couple a fraction of the unknown power to a thermistor or bolometer bridge. This method also allows the forward and reflected powers to be measured separately. In many cases it is also more convenient to measure high powers by this method, as it leaves the original system virtually undisturbed, as far as the power level is concerned, and does not require the elaboration of water supplies, etc.

Radiation pressure wattmeters

A range of wattmeters [4] have been developed that measure power by using the mechanical force, or torque, exerted by the electric or magnetic fields in the waveguide, on a small vane. These devices are absolute in the sense that they can be calibrated in terms of the restoring couple, exerted by the suspension system on which the vane is mounted, and a simple microwave experiment involving the measurement of distance only.

A vane wattmeter which effectively measures the electric field strength in the guide is shown in Fig. 11.7. The reflection from the

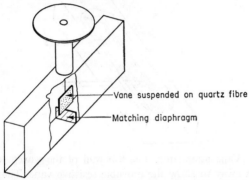

Vane suspended on quartz fibre

Matching diaphragm

Figure 11.7. Vane wattmeter. Part of the waveguide wall has been cut away to show the vane suspended from the torsion head and the matching diaphragm.

diaphragm, which is capacitive, is matched by an inductive diaphragm. As the device is electric field operated it will only measure correctly the power into a matched load. By using two vanes spaced by a quarter wavelength the device can measure power into a mismatched load. Various other versions of this device have been produced.

Their main disadvantage is that the very small torque produced for powers in the region of 1–100 W necessitates suspending the vane on a thin quartz fibre. Thus the instrument is very delicate and has to be carefully levelled.

Calibrated attenuators, phase shifters and short circuits

Calibrated variable attenuators

Vane type. The basic construction of variable waveguide attenuators is quite simple. A strip of lossy material is introduced into the waveguide so that the electric field is parallel to the surface of the strip. As the electric field varies over the cross section of the guide the amount of loss and hence the attenuation can be controlled by altering the position of the strip. The arrangement for a TE_{01} guide is shown in Fig. 11.8. The resistive strip is usually a thin glass plate coated with a film of evaporated metal such as Nichrome. The device has to be calibrated initially and careful design of both the mechanical arrangements that move the strip and the lossy strip itself ensure that the calibration is maintained. Fixed attenuators

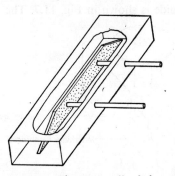

Figure 11.8. Vane attenuator. The top wall of the waveguide has been partially cut away to show the movable resistive vane. The micrometer drive that operates the vane is not shown.

may be made by omitting the adjusting mechanism. Reflections are avoided by tapering the ends of the resistive strip.

Vane attenuators in co-axial cable may be made but as the attenuation varies widely with frequency they are not as satisfactory as piston attenuators.

Piston type. The evanescent fields in a waveguide, operated beyond cut-off, fall off exponentially with distance along the guide. This rapid attenuation may be used to form a variable attenuator. A waveguide mode is launched by a probe mounted in a circular guide that is well beyond cut-off. A movable pick-up probe provides the output. Due to the exponential field variation the attenuation is a linear function of the distance between the launching and pick-up probes. This mechanism is widely used in signal generators but the small size of the guide necessary for it to be beyond cut-off, above about 6 GHz, makes the piston attenuator unsatisfactory for the upper end of the microwave band.

Rotary attenuator

In this device [5] a lossy vane is mounted in a circular waveguide carrying a polarized TE_{11} mode. Two fixed resistive vanes ensure that only one plane of polarization exists whilst transition sections enable

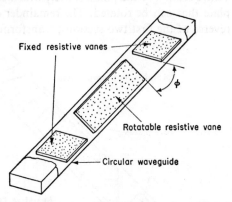

Figure 11.9. Rotary attenuator. The attenuator is constructed in circular waveguide with transitions to standard rectangular waveguide at each end.

the attenuator to be coupled to rectangular waveguide. One advantage of this guide is that the vane absorbs all the electric field components parallel to its surface so that if the vane is rotated the attenuation is directly related to the angular position of the vane. The instrument does not require calibration and is not frequency sensitive. It is illustrated in Fig. 11.9.

Electrically operated attenuators

See Chapter 9, p. 136.

Phase shifters

Waveguide type. Variable waveguide phase shifters can be made by arranging a piece of low loss dielectric so that it can be moved across the waveguide in much the same manner as the resistive strip is moved in the case of the variable attenuator. Again precautions must be taken to prevent reflections occurring from the dielectric strip.

Rotary phase shifter. This device [6] operates in circular guide using the TE_{11} mode and is shown to Fig. 11.10. A taper is used to transform from the normal rectangular guide to the circular pipe and a resistive card section ensures the correct plane of polarization. A quarter wavelength plate is placed at 45° to the plane of polarization so that the component of the field parallel to it is retarded by $\pi/2$, compared with the normal component. Thus circular polarization exists in the centre section of the phase shifter, which contains a half wavelength plate that can be rotated. The remainder of the instrument is the reverse of the first two sections, transforming back first

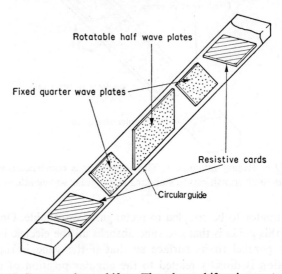

Figure 11.10. Rotary phase shifter. The phase shifter is constructed in circular guide with tapers to rectangular guide at each end. See text for positioning of the fixed plates.

to plane polarization in the circular guide and then back to rectangular guide. The rotable half-wavelength section changes the phase of the wave having an electric field parallel to its surface by π. The resulting combination of components parallel to, and normal to, the half-wave plate results in a wave, still circularly polarized, but shifted in phase by 2θ, where θ is the angle through which the half-wave plate has been turned. Thus, if the plate is rotated through 180°, the phase change through device is 360°. The use of quarter-wave and half-wave plates makes the device frequency sensitive.

Co-axial line type. Telescopic sections of co-axial line known as line stretchers may be used to obtain phase shifts in co-axial cable systems. It is often convenient to combine two such sections in a trombone line so that the two connections to the phase shifter remain stationary.

Adjustable short circuits

The adjustable short circuit is useful for many purposes and provides a susceptance standard for microwave measurements. As the impedance of a short circuited line is given by

$$Z = jZ_0 \tan \frac{2\pi z}{\lambda_g}$$

the actual value of the susceptance may be known if the distance between the plunger and the end of the line is accurately known. A scale or micrometer drive is provided for this purpose.

It is also essential that the short circuit should have a reflection

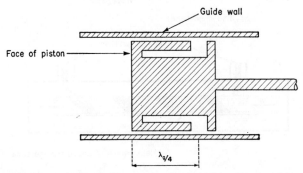

Figure 11.11. Non-contact plunger. The double-quarter wave slot presents a short circuit at the face of the plunger even though there is no contact with the guide walls.

coefficient nearly equal to unity. The movable short circuit is usually fitted with spring fingers so that it makes good contact with the walls and inner of the co-axial cable, or the walls of the waveguide. In the case of waveguide and co-axial line short circuits, if the device is to be used over a limited pass-band, then a choke design has to be used in which the use of quarter-wavelength sections enables a non-contact piston to be used. This is shown in Fig. 11.11.

Noise measurement

The basic method of measurement of noise in the microwave region consists of using a standard noise source. Two basic sources are used

M

in the microwave region. Firstly, a body at a known temperature may be used as a source. As the melting point of most material that may be conveniently heated, e.g. tungsten filaments, is limited to about 2,800° K the maximum noise output is quite small (corresponding to about 10 db max) and only low noise devices can be conveniently compared to these devices. However, both heated wire

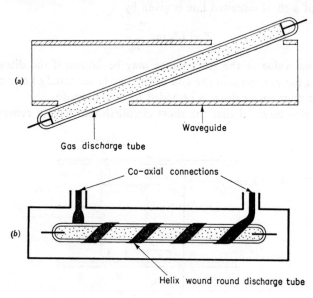

Figure 11.12(a). Waveguide noise source. The tube is placed at a shallow angle to the guide and is thus matched to the guide.
Figure 11.12(b) Co-axial noise source. A helix is wound round the discharge tube and terminated in co-axial sockets.

sources and even boiling water loads have been used as noise standards. The source must, of course, be matched to the transmission system in which it is placed.

A more commonly used source is an argon discharge tube. This is matched to a waveguide by mounting it as shown in Fig. 11.12(a), or to a co-axial system as in Fig. 11.12(b). The noise source figure of such a tube is 11,400° K or 15·8 db and is almost independent of the operating condition of the tube.

The usual method of noise measurement is to note the noise output from the device under test with its input connected to a matched load at room temperature. The input is then connected to the discharge tube noise source via a variable attenuator and the attenuator adjusted until the noise output of the device is doubled. The noise figure, or temperature, of the device is then equal to that of the noise output from the attenuator. In practice non-linearity in the detector is often a problem and it may be convenient to put a 3 db attenuator in the detector and adjust for the same output reading, thus avoiding the problem.

In the absence of a noise source a signal generator may be used but this requires a knowledge of the bandwidth of the system under test. Automatic noise figure meters have been developed for rapid noise measurements.

The measurement of very low noise figures presents some difficulties, as attenuation due to components at room temperature forms an additional source of noise. Also discontinuities in the system are troublesome. A very simple noise measurement system that avoids some of these troubles is that in which the input of the device is connected to a matched load at room temperature and the noise output noted. The load is then cooled in liquid nitrogen and the noise output again noted, or the detector attenuation adjusted to give the same reading (i.e. the attenuation in the detector is reduced).

The calculation of noise from the above experiments is self-apparent from the basic definition of noise figure.

$$\text{Noise figure} = \frac{\begin{array}{c}\text{Actual noise output from actual device} \\ \text{with input load at room temperature}\end{array}}{\begin{array}{c}\text{Noise output from ideal amplifier of same} \\ \text{gain with input load at room temperature}\end{array}}$$

$$= \frac{\text{Noise output (input at } T_0)}{GkT_0B}$$

$$= \frac{\text{Excess noise from device} + GkT_0B}{GkT_0B}$$

Thus by making measurements of the actual noise output for two values of input load temperature the noise figure can be found.

Frequency measurements

Wavemeters

At low r.f. wavemeters using tuned lumped resonant circuits are used and these may be used up to a few hundred Mc/s. Above this the tuned circuit is a co-axial line or waveguide short circuited so that its length is $n\lambda_g/2$. By making the short circuit at one end adjustable the device may be adjusted to tune over a range of frequencies and the low loss of the waveguide results in a high Q device. Co-axial cable or rectangular waveguide may be used but both these necessitate a tuning plunger that makes contact with the wall of the line. It is preferable to use a circular waveguide operating in the TE_{01} mode as the short circuit can then be a non-contact plunger. A suitable

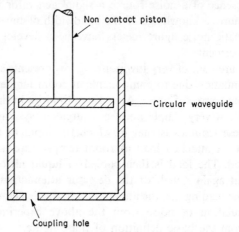

Figure 11.13. Cavity wavemeter. A coupling hole is shown here but a coupling loop may also be used.

arrangement is shown in Fig. 11.13. The resonant cavity formed by the shorted guide is loosely coupled to the circuit under test. Resonance may be detected either by noticing the reduction in the power in the main circuit or by an auxiliary detector coupled to the cavity.

Due to the high Q obtainable accurate frequency discrimination is possible if care is taken in the mechanical design. However the cavity can operate in a number of modes other than the TE_{01} mode and it will resonate when it is $n\lambda_g/2$ in length for any of these modes. If the rough value of the frequency is not known care must be taken not to obtain an incorrect value of the frequency due to the cavity operating in a mode other than the one it was calibrated for.

Standard frequency sources

Atomic frequency standards. The most accurate frequency standards use atomic resonance. If there is any transition from one energy state to another, then there is an absorption, or emission of energy, at a frequency given by

$$F_{12} = \frac{E_1 - E_2}{h}$$

h = Planck's constant

E_1, E_2 are the energy levels of the two states concerned.

There are many different forms of energy states and only certain

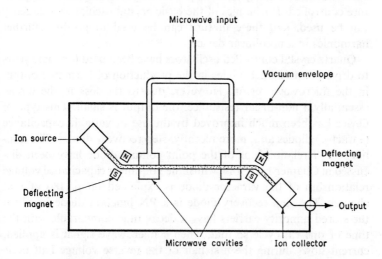

Figure 11.14. Cesium atomic frequency standard.

state energy differences give frequencies in the microwave band. One such is the magnetic dipole transition in cesium. The 4·3, 3·0 transition in cesium corresponds to a frequency of 9·19263177 GHz. The arrangement is shown in Fig. 11.14.

A cesium oven produces a beam of cesium vapour, which is passed through a magnetic field gradient which separates the different magnetic energy states. The selected beam then passes through the double cavity arrangement, which is a means of producing the effect of a long cavity, thus avoiding the difficulties encountered when using a physically long cavity, and then passes through a second state separator. Atoms that have made transitions are then deflected to a detector. These transitions are a maximum when the signal applied to the cavity is exactly that corresponding to the energy state difference.

The whole system is contained in an evacuated tube and complete, commercially available, time standards are made. The frequency stability is about three parts in 10^{12} over long periods.

Standards using atomic hydrogen, rubidium gas and ammonia gas have also been used.

Quartz crystal standards. For many years quartz crystal oscillators have been used as radio frequency standards. Although not absolute such standards are very reliable, particularly if the crystal is temperature controlled. Harmonics of the basic crystal oscillation frequency can be used, and these in turn can be used to produce further harmonics in a non-linear device.

Quartz crystal controlled oscillators have been used for some years to drive point contact diodes in the production of harmonic output in the microwave region. However, due to the loss in the diode, essentially a non-linear resistance, the output is small. This type of device has been much improved by the use of variable capacitance (varactor) diodes and, more recently, step recovery diodes. The non-linear V/I relationships of the point contact diode have been discussed in Chapter 12, p. 184, whilst the non-linear capacitance voltage relationship of the varactor diode is explained on p. 180 of that chapter. The step recovery diode is a PN junction diode in which the stored minority carriers have a decay time comparable with the time of one r.f. cycle so that, when a microwave signal is applied, current flows during the first half of the reverse voltage half cycle but ceases very abruptly when the store of charge carriers is used up. This rapid cessation of current constitutes a waveform, rich in harmonic content, and reasonable output may be extracted at anything up to the twentieth harmonic. This type of diode should be contrasted with the varactor where the harmonic content falls off quite rapidly with the harmonic number, and where each diode can only be used, efficiently, to multiply by two or three times. The current waveform for a charge storage diode is shown in Fig. 12.2. The diode itself is a normal PN junction with the doping densities chosen to make the decay time a reasonable fraction of the fundamental operating frequency.

Swept frequency measurements and spectrum analysers

It is usually required to know the properties of a system, or component, over a fairly wide range of frequencies, and point by point measurements over a wide band are slow and tedious and may possibly miss any very rapid change of the measured property with frequency. Swept frequency techniques are now very widely used for measurements. The most important component of the swept frequency system is a signal source that will sweep rapidly over the required range and, preferably, give a constant power output over this range.

A reflex klystron oscillator can be swept by mechanically adjusting its cavity and at the same time arranging that the reflector voltage is adjusted to maintain resonance. Only slow sweep rates are possible, due to the use of a mechanical system, and it is preferable to use a backward wave oscillator as the source, as this can be electronically tuned by controlling its line voltage. Unfortunately, the power output of a BWO varies rather drastically if only its line voltage is adjusted but this may be compensated for by simultaneously adjusting the beam current by means of a grid in the electron gun. A reasonably constant output, within a db, may be obtained by this method. However by using a PIN attenuator (see Chapter 9) the output may be further levelled electronically to give an output that is within about 0·1 db over the whole swept range.

Swept frequency reflectometers

The swept frequency source is used in conjunction with the reflectometer described on p. 158. If the power output of the oscillator varies, then the output from the forward and backward wave outputs of the directional coupler must be compared with a ratio meter and displayed on an oscilloscope. However, where PIN attenuators are used to level the forward wave power then reflected wave power may be directly displayed. This type of display is extremely useful when attempting to match components over a broad band.

Automatic reflection coefficient plotters

By using a swept frequency source in conjunction with automatic measurement of both s.w.r. and minima position (phase of reflection coefficient), and a suitable display system, plots of the complex reflection coefficient over a frequency band may be displayed. The simple reflectometer technique does not give phase information and the reflection coefficient plotters use either two couplers, or a series of waveguide probes, or a specially coupled circular auxiliary guide where the forward and backward waves produce waves in the auxiliary guide of opposite polarization. In the latter case, both the phase and amplitude of the reflection coefficient can be obtained by rotating a polarized detector in the auxiliary guide.

Spectrum analysers

By making a receiver that has a very narrow bandwidth and which sweeps continuously over a frequency range the frequency spectrum of a signal may be displayed and analysed. Until fairly recently frequency sweeping was achieved either by electronic tuning of klystron oscillators, which gives only a narrow swept band, or mechanical klystron tuning, which is clumsy and slow. However, the availability of voltage tuned BWO's has enabled very versatile spectrum analysers to be made.

In a typical analyser, a BWO is used as a local oscillator to sweep over a 2 GHz range and a relatively high IF frequency, about 2 GHz, is used to eliminate image frequency responses. The instrument can be used directly to analyse signals from 10 GHz to a few GHz using a co-axial input. By using an external waveguide mixer, the instrument can be used up to 40 GHz.

Voltage measurements

In co-axial systems it is possible to measure voltage directly at the lower end of the microwave spectrum. Fairly accurate measurements may be made up to about 1 GHz and indications obtained up to 5 GHz. A conventional form of diode voltmeter is used with a special diode and diode mount.

Diode voltmeter measurements are limited at high frequencies by the finite transit time of electrons in the cathode anode space of the diode, and by the self-resonant frequency, due to the interelectrode capacitance of the diode together with the inductance of its lead. By using very close spacing between the cathode and anode, the transit time can be made small enough to make useful measurements in the microwave region. However, the very close spacing makes the capacitance per unit cathode area of the diode rather high so small cathodes have to be used. The diode probe unit is inserted in a special co-axial mount which has a s.w.r. of about 1·2 up to 1 GHz. Ideally, measurements should be confined to frequencies below the self-resonant frequency of the voltmeter but tolerable measurement can be made around or above this frequency, provided a correction is made for this error.

The sampling oscilloscope

The maximum frequency of operation of a cathode ray tube is severely limited by its deflector plate system. The time taken for the electron beam to pass through the vertical deflector plates must be small compared with the r.f. period and, using beams with a velocity corresponding to a few kilovolts, this necessitates using extremely short deflector plates if the system is to respond to signals in the microwave band. However, a short deflector plate system is very

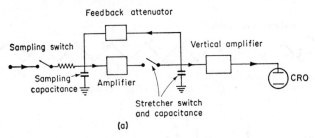

Figure 11.15(a). Sampling switch, stretcher switch, feedback mechanism and vertical amplifier for sampling oscilloscope.

insensitive and, to make matters worse, high gain, wide band amplifiers that have a frequency response extending right up to the microwave region are almost impossible to make, and any practical system would have to use a series of amplifiers, each covering only an octave or so of bandwidth. The problem of making a very high frequency oscilloscope that falls within an acceptable price range has been solved by using the sampling technique. The sampling system is shown in Fig. 11.15. A very high speed semiconductor switch is closed for an extremely short time and thus charges the sampling capacitor. As the switch is closed for a very short time, the capacitor is only charged to about 5% of the applied voltage, but the resulting signal is then amplified and used to charge a second capacitor via the stretcher switch which closes synchronously with the sampling switch but remains closed for a relatively long time. The voltage from the stretcher capacitor is amplified sufficiently to operate the vertical plates of a conventional cathode ray tube. At the same time a signal is fed back to the sampling capacitor which charges it to

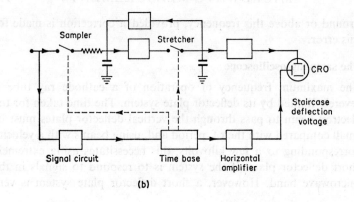

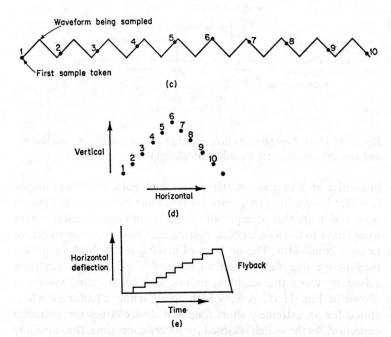

Figure 11.15(b). Complete sampling oscilloscope system.

Figure 11.15(c). Waveform being sampled at regular intervals.

Figure 11.15(d). CRO display of sampled signal. Amplitude of sampled signal is represented by vertical position of spot.

Figure 11.15(e). Horizontal deflection by staircase signal.

100% of the original sampled signal (it only charged to about 5% during the time the sampling switch was closed). Thus, when a second sample is taken, only the difference in voltage will be recorded.

The sampling switch is operated by a command signal from the time base that supplies the horizontal plates of the CRO. This horizontal time base is a staircase generator and deflects the electron beam in a series of steps. At each step the sampling switch, and also the stretcher switch, are closed so that a voltage is fed to the vertical plate which represents the amplitude of the sample taken. The combination of the synchronizing circuit and the time base result in samples being taken at various points in the r.f. cycle, and the stored samples being displayed, at comparatively slow speeds, on a conventional cathode ray tube. To enable the signal to be presented as a conventional plot of voltage against time, the stored signal on the stretcher capacitor is arranged to give a single spot on the face of the tube, the height of the spot above the zero voltage axis representing the voltage at the time of sampling.

As the sampling time has to be short compared with the period the circuitry problems connected with the sampling switch and its controlling time base are extremely difficult and there is insufficient space to discuss them here. The various diagrams in Fig. 11.15 indicate the essential mode of operation.

References

[1] *J.A.P.*, 1946, **17**, 610.
[2] *Trans. I.R.E.*, 1953, **24**, 1046.
[3] *J.A.P.*, 1946, **17**, 530.
[4] *Proc. I.E.E.*, 1952, **99**, 294.
[5] *Electronics*, 1954, **27**, 184.
[6] *Proc. I.R.E.*, 1948, **26**, 245.

General

E. L. Gintzen, *Microwave Measurements*, McGraw-Hill Book Co., 1957.
H. M. Barlow and A. L. Cullen, *Microwave Measurements*, Constable and Co., 1950.

CHAPTER 12

Semiconductor Devices for Passive Microwave Components

A wide range of semiconductor devices are used in microwave systems but only those used in passive components will be considered here.

At lower frequencies a large number of semiconductor devices are based on the voltage variable resistance characteristic of the PN junction but in the microwave region, it is not possible to use this characteristic and other effects, or other forms of diode are used.

In a PN junction there is a depletion layer, virtually devoid of mobile charges between the P and N regions, and the width of this depletion layer is a function of the applied bias voltage. There is also a contact potential that appears across the depletion layer. The depletion layer thus acts very much like a dielectric between the two conducting regions and, as the width of this region is a function of voltage, the device behaves as a voltage variable capacitance. For an abrupt junction this capacitance is given by

$$C_J = A \left[2q \, \varepsilon \, \frac{V_0 - V}{\dfrac{1}{N_D} + \dfrac{1}{N_A}} \right]^{\frac{1}{2}} \tag{12.1}$$

where N_A, N_D are acceptor and donor densities, V_0 is the contact potential, V is the applied potential, q is the electron charge, ε the semi-conductor permittivity and A the junction area.

Application of a bias voltage to the diode, in addition to changing the capacitance, causes current to flow through the diode. The majority carriers in the P and N regions have to cross the depletion layer against the effect of the contact potential, and can only do so if they have sufficient thermal energy. As the thermal energy has approximately a Boltzmann distribution, any change in the applied voltage, and hence the total field across the depletion region, alters the proportion of majority carriers that have sufficient energy to cross the barrier, and thus alters the current. Minority carriers that reach the edge of the depletion region are swept across the region by the field. For large reverse bias conditions, the junction current is essentially composed of these minority carriers. The resulting total current is given by

$$I = I_s(e^{qV/kT} - 1) \tag{12.2}$$

where I_s is the reverse saturation current, V the applied bias, q the electronic charge and k Boltzmann's constant.

Thus the depletion layer can be represented by a voltage variable capacitance, in parallel with a voltage variable resistance. However, the connecting terminals of the diode are not placed at the edges of the depletion layer but are attached to the ends of the bulk material. Thus, there is the resistance of the bulk material, in series with the junction impedance, and the equivalent circuit is as shown in Fig. 12.1.

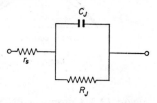

Figure 12.1. General equivalent circuit of PN junction diode.

The combination of the series resistance and the depletion layer capacitance presents serious problems in the microwave region if the non-linear resistance properties of the device are to be exploited. In the forward direction the minimum resistance is limited by the series resistance, whilst for reverse bias the diode is shunted by the reactance of the depletion layer capacitance. Thus the greatest ratio of backward to forward impedance that can be obtained, even if the backward/forward resistance ratio of the depletion layer itself is infinite, is given by

$$Z_B/Z_F = \frac{r_s + \dfrac{1}{j\omega C_b}}{r_s} = 1 + \frac{1}{j\omega C_b r_s}$$

It is obvious that the $r_s C_b$ product is a serious limiting factor when the non-linear properties of the diode are required. When the frequency is such that $\omega C_b r_s \ll 1$, then the diode has virtually the same impedance in the forward and backward directions.

As for a given type of diode the series resistance is inversely proportional to the cross-junction area and the depletion layer capacitance directly proportional, the $r_s C_b$ product of a diode cannot be reduced by reducing the junction area. However it can be reduced by another technique as will be shown in the next section.

So far only the static characteristics of the diode have been considered. When the dynamic effects are considered, it is found that the charge storage effect seriously affects the microwave properties of a PN diode. When the majority carriers cross the depletion region, under the influence of forward bias, they then enter the opposite side of the junction and become minority carriers. The density of the

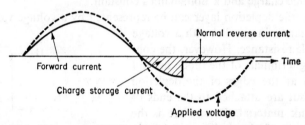

Figure 12.2. Current in PN junction when period of applied voltage is comparable with the storage time.

injected carriers decays exponentially with a time constant that does not usually exceed 10^{-8} s. If the applied bias is reversed during this period then the injected carriers will return across the depletion region and constitute a pulse of reverse current in excess of that given by the static characteristic, equation (12.2). The resulting waveform is shown in Fig. 12.2. In the microwave region the time constant for decay is considerably longer than the period and so the diode is useless as a rectifier or mixer. However, the very rapid fall of reverse current that occurs when all the stored carriers have returned across the depletion region or recombined is rich in harmonics of the applied frequency, and this phenomenon may be used for frequency multiplication.

The varactor (variable capacitance diode)

If a PN junction is reverse biased and the reverse bias current is very small, then the diode equivalent circuit is virtually that of a voltage variable capacitance in series with the resistance of the bulk material. Provided that the reactance of the depletion layer greatly exceeds the series resistance, then the device can be used as a variable reactance.

Varactor diodes are designed to have very small reverse currents and their maximum usable frequency is related to their cut-off frequency given by

$$\omega_c = \frac{1}{r_s C_J}$$

For the varactor to be reasonably pure reactance the operating frequency must not exceed about $\frac{1}{10}$ of the cut-off frequency. Varactors are available with cut-off frequencies up to 500 GHz and so they may be used up to about 50 GHz. In order to keep the varactor capacitance small enough to be included in normal microwave circuits the junction area of the varactor has to be quite small and hence the power handling capacity is limited. The voltage swing is limited also by the reverse breakdown voltage of the diode. Some details of the power handling capabilities of switches and phase shifters using varactors are given in Chapter 9.

The PIN diode

In this diode the P and N regions are separated by an intrinsic region. Carriers leaving the doped regions have to cross this intrinsic region to reach the opposite side of the junction and the time they take to do so is such that the diode ceases to act as an efficient rectifier for frequencies in excess of about 100 MHz, and in the micro-

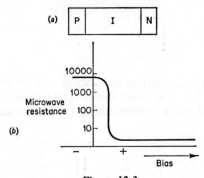

Figure 12.3.

(*a*) PIN diode.

(*b*) Variation of microwave resistance of PIN diode with applied bias.

wave region the diode then appears as a linear resistance. However, if a d.c. bias signal is applied to the diode in addition to the microwave system, then the number of carriers injected into the intrinsic region, and hence its effective resistance, is greatly affected by the injection current. The conductivity of the intrinsic region can be varied by a factor of several thousand by the injected current. The construction of the diode and its microwave properties are shown in Fig. 12.3.

The point contact diode

From the inception of microwaves until quite recently, the point contact diode has been the only device capable of acting as an efficient mixer and detector. The diode consists of a thin metal wire, sharpened at one end, whose point rests on a small silicon chip. The metal/semi-conductor junction has a voltage current characteristic similar to that of a PN junction, but, as one of the materials is a metal, the charge storage problem is not as serious as it is in the PN diode. Furthermore the problem of the fixed $r_s C_J$ product is overcome by the point contact structure. The bulk material through which the current has to flow is now of the form of a truncated pyramid, the junction with the metal wire forming the top of the device. Whereas for a planar diode the resistance of the bulk material is inversely proportional to the area, in the case of a device of circular cross-section proportional to $1/\text{radius}^2$ in the case of a truncated cone, the resistance is related to $1/\text{radius}$, the radius being that at the metal semiconductor junction. In both the planar and point contact devices the

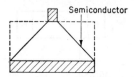

Figure 12.4. Spreading resistance of truncated cone. In practice the semiconductor would have the shape shown by the dotted outline but the current flow would still be confined mainly to the cone-shaped part of the material.

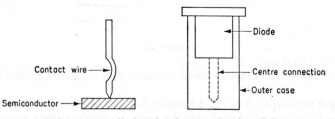

Figure 12.5. Point contact diode. The sharpened point of the contact wire is pressed against the semiconductor.

junction capacitance is controlled by (radius)². Hence in the point contact diode the r_sC_J product *can* be reduced by reducing the radius of the contact. The term r_s in the case of the point contact diode is frequently referred to as the spreading resistance, as the current spreads out from the small point contact to the relatively large connection to the silicon chip. Fig. 12.4 illustrates this effect.

Point contact diodes are either mounted in a package of the form shown in Fig. 12.5 or, for millimetre wavelengths, they are mounted

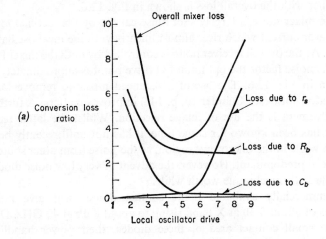

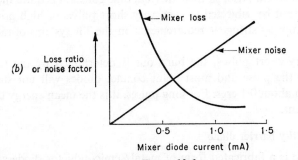

Figure 12.6.

(*a*) Variation of loss in a mixer diode for varying local oscillator drive. The losses due to C_b, R_b and r_s are shown separately together with the total loss.

(*b*) Variation of loss and noise figure as a function of diode current. At high frequencies the noise is virtually all due to shot noise and hence rises linearly with increase in the rectified diode current.

N

in a short section of waveguide which is inserted in the main waveguide run.

When the point contact diode is used as a mixer, the two most important features of the mixer are its loss and its noise figure. Both these factors are largely controlled by the diode itself, together with the amplitude of the local oscillator drive. The losses in the mixer are caused by the actual barrier resistance, the barrier capacitance and the spreading resistance. Variation of both these individual losses together with the overall loss is shown in Fig. 12.6.

The mixer noise is largely shot noise caused by the rectified local oscillator current which rises almost linearly with the local oscillator drive. As the overall receiver noise is controlled by both the mixer loss and its noise factor the optimum LO drive point is approximately as shown in Fig. 12.6. The use of a balanced mixer to remove local oscillator noise (see Chapter 10, p. 142) improves matters. A further improvement is the use of image rejection. Whilst the latter technique has been known for some time, it has not until recently been worth while in the microwave region, as the noise from other sources has been predominant. However, the advent of very low noise diodes has made this technique worth while.

Commercially available point contact diodes will give noise figures of about 6 db at X band rising to about 8 db at 40 GHz. Due to the small contact area of these diodes, their power handling capacity is small. Also, as their thermal time constant is quite short, they must not be subjected to even very short pulses of high power and this imposes stringent requirements on the TR systems of radar sets.

For very short pulses, the burn out is determined by the total energy in the pulse and most point contact diodes will not stand more than about 0·1 ergs. For long pulses, it is the mean energy that is important.

The Schottky barrier diode

This diode is a fabricated form of metal/semiconductor diode and, like the point contact diode, avoids the problems of charge storage and fixed $r_s C_J$ product. The construction of the diode is shown in Fig. 12.7. A very small hole is etched in the oxide layer and metal is deposited through the hole to make contact with the semiconductor. This form of construction is much more controllable than that of the point contact diode, and gallium arsenide diodes of this form have given noise figures of 5 db at X band. It is hoped to obtain figures of 3–4 db in the near future.

The single pulse burn-out capability of Schottky barrier diodes is

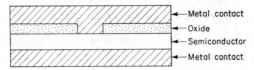

Figure 12.7. Schottky barrier diode.

several times higher than that of point contact diodes and is typically five ergs.

This type of diode shows great promise since by feeding the signal directly into a mixer using this type of diode, noise figures may be obtained which are as good as those obtained using a point contact mixer diode and a pre-amplifier.

APPENDIX

Spin resonance and the effects arising from it

We will first consider a single electron spinning in a magnetic field. Due to the magnetic dipole effect of the spinning electron it will normally align itself with the applied field. If the electron is disturbed it will precess about its normal position in the manner of a mechanical gyroscope. The arrangement is shown in Fig. A1.

Let the angular momentum vector, p, make an angle θ with the vertical and precess about a cone with an angular velocity

$$\frac{\mathrm{d}\phi}{\mathrm{d}t} = \omega_0$$

The time rate of change of angular momentum equals the torque which may be written

$$\frac{\mathrm{d}p}{\mathrm{d}t} = T \tag{A1}$$

In a time interval $\mathrm{d}t$ the change in angular momentum is $T\mathrm{d}t$ and the change ϕ is $\mathrm{d}\phi$. Also $\mathrm{d}\phi$ is equal to the arc $T\mathrm{d}t$ divided by the radius of the precession circle $p \sin \theta$. From this we obtain

$$\frac{\mathrm{d}\phi}{\mathrm{d}t} = \omega_0 = \frac{T}{p \sin \theta} \tag{A2}$$

and from (A1)

$$\frac{\mathrm{d}p}{\mathrm{d}t} = \omega_0 \, p \sin \theta \tag{A3}$$

or in vector form

$$\frac{\mathrm{d}p}{\mathrm{d}t} = \boldsymbol{\omega}_0 \times p \tag{A4}$$

This is the equation of motion for the angular momentum vector. The magnetic moment of the spinning electron μ_e is parallel to the angular momentum vector and the ratio of the magnetic moment to the angular momentum is known as the gyromagnetic ratio

$$\gamma = -\frac{\mu_e}{p} \tag{A5}$$

The potential energy, U, of a magnetic dipole in a magnetic dipole in a uniform field H is given by

$$U = \mu_e H \cos \theta \qquad (A6)$$

As the torque T is related to U by

$$T = -\frac{dU}{d\theta} \qquad (A7)$$

where the negative sign arises because the magnetic moment and the angular momentum vector are oppositely directed in a spinning electron, equation (6) may be used here to give $T = \mu_e H \sin \theta$.

Rewriting (7) in vector form

$$\frac{d\boldsymbol{p}}{dt} = T = \boldsymbol{\mu}_e \times \mathbf{H} \qquad (A8)$$

Substituting from (5) gives

$$\frac{d\boldsymbol{p}}{dt} = -\gamma(\boldsymbol{p} \times \mathbf{H}) = \gamma(\mathbf{H} \times \boldsymbol{p}) = \boldsymbol{\omega}_0 \times \boldsymbol{p} \qquad (A9)$$

and by analogy with (4)

$$\omega_0 = \gamma H \qquad (A10)$$

This is the natural precessional angular frequency for a spinning electron in a magnetic field.

If there are N dipoles per unit volume and they are all aligned in a parallel manner (this is true for a ferromagnetic material but not for a ferrimagnetic one) then the total magnetic moment per unit volume is

$$M = N\mu_e \qquad (A11)$$

Hence from (5) and (8)

$$\frac{dM}{dt} = -\gamma(M \times \mathbf{H}) \qquad (A12)$$

This is now the macroscopic differential equation of motion for the magnetic moment M.

Resonance condition

Consider now the application of a time-varying field given by

$$\mathbf{H} = \mathbf{H}_0 + \boldsymbol{h}e^{j\omega t} \qquad (A13)$$

Resonance occurs when $\omega = \omega_0$.

If the relative directions of the a.c. and d.c. components of the applied magnetic field are as shown in Fig. A2 then, at resonance, the amplitude of the precession will grow steadily and energy will be absorbed from the applied a.c. field. The alternating components of magnetization can be written as

$$M = M_0 + me^{j\omega t} \tag{A14}$$

and we will assume that $H_0 \gg h$ so that $M_0 \gg m$.

If we insert (A13) and (A14) into (A11) and expand, ignoring products of small quantities h and m, the resultant has two components, a. d.c. term and an a.c. term. These are for the d.c. term

$$\gamma(M_0 \times H_0) = 0 \tag{A15}$$

and for the a.c. term $j\omega m = (M_0 \times h + m \times H_0)$ (A16)

Multiplying (A16) vectorially by H_0 gives

$$j\omega m \times H_0 = \gamma(M_0 \times h) \times H_0 + \gamma(m \times H_0) \times H_0 \tag{A17}$$

and expanding using the identity

$$A \times (B \times C) = (A.C)B - (A.B)C$$

we obtain

$$j\omega m \times H_0 = \gamma(H_0 . M_0)h - \gamma(H_0 . h)M_0$$
$$+ \gamma(H_0 . m)H_0 - \gamma(H_0 . H_0)m \tag{A18}$$

However taking the *scalar* product of (A16) and H_0 gives

$$H_0 . j\omega m = \gamma(M_0 \times h)H_0 + \gamma(m \times H_0)H_0$$
$$= h.\gamma(H_0 \times M_0) + m.\gamma(H_0 \times M_0) \tag{A19}$$

And as (A15) gives $\gamma(H_0 + M_0) = 0$ (A19) becomes

$$j\omega m H_0 = 0 \tag{A20}$$

and as $\omega \neq 0$ it follows that $m . H_0 = 0$.

Thus the r.f. magnetization is perpendicular to H_0 to a first order. Also the third term in the RHS of (A18) vanishes and we may solve for m to give

$$m = \frac{1}{(\omega_0{}^2 - \omega^2)}[j\omega\gamma(M_0 \times h) + \gamma^2(H_0.M_0)h - \gamma^2(H_0.h)M_0] \tag{A21}$$

Obviously the resonance condition is a critical one as when

$$\omega = \omega_0 = \gamma H_0 \tag{A22}$$

then $m = \infty$.

We have used the terms normally used in magnetic work for the above consideration but it is apparent that if the magnetization tends to infinity then the permeability does likewise. It is convenient to write the susceptibility of the material in tensor form and we can do this by examining (A21). Assume that the co-ordinate system is such that H_0 and M_0 lie along the z axis and consider the applied a.c. field to be of the form

$$h = ih_x + jh_y + kh_z$$

where i, j, k are the unit vectors in the x, y and z directions. Then we can write by inspection of (A20)

$$m_x = \frac{\gamma M_0}{\omega_0{}^2 - \omega^2}(\omega_0 h_x - j\omega h_y) \tag{A23}$$

$$m_y = \frac{\gamma M_0}{\omega_0{}^2 - \omega^2}(j\omega h_x + \omega_0 h_y) \tag{A24}$$

$$m_z = 0 \tag{A25}$$

Remembering that the d.c. magnetization is the saturation value M, all the spins are initially aligned with the d.c. fields and the permeability for frequencies well removed from gyromagnetic resonance is substantially equal to that of free space.

The susceptibility tensor is written as $\boldsymbol{m} = \chi \cdot \boldsymbol{h}$

$$\chi = \begin{bmatrix} \chi_{xx} & \chi_{xy} & 0 \\ \chi_{yx} & \chi_{yy} & 0 \\ 0 & 0 & 0 \end{bmatrix} \tag{A26}$$

and from (A23) to (A25)

$$\chi_{xx} = \chi_{yy} = \frac{\omega_0 \omega_M}{\omega_0{}^2 - \omega^2} \tag{A27}$$

$$\chi_{xy} = \chi_{yx} = \frac{j\omega \omega_M}{\omega_0{}^2 - \omega^2} \tag{A28}$$

$$\omega_M = 4\pi\gamma M_0 \tag{A29}$$

The permeability tensor is then

$$\boldsymbol{\mu} = \mu_0 \begin{bmatrix} \mu & -j\kappa & 0 \\ j\kappa & \mu & 0 \\ 0 & 0 & 1 \end{bmatrix} \tag{A30}$$

where $\mu = 1 + \chi_{xx}$, $j\kappa = -\chi_{xy}$
and the relation between the flux density and the magnetic field is

$$\boldsymbol{B} = \boldsymbol{\mu}\boldsymbol{H} \tag{A31}$$

$$\mu = 1 + \frac{4\pi M_0 H_0 \gamma^2}{\gamma^2 H_0 - \omega^2} \tag{A32}$$

and

$$\kappa = \frac{4\pi\omega\gamma M_0}{\gamma^2 H_0{}^2 - \omega^2} \tag{A33}$$

So far we have followed the convention used in magnetic problems and used Gaussian units. In MKS units the values of μ and κ are

$$\mu = 1 + \frac{\gamma^2 H_0 \dfrac{M_0}{\mu_0}}{\gamma^2 H_0^2 - \omega^2} \tag{A.34}$$

$$\kappa = \frac{\omega\gamma \dfrac{M_0}{\mu_0}}{\gamma^2 H_0^2 - \omega^2} \tag{A35}$$

and hence

$$B_x = \mu_0(\mu h_x - j\kappa h_y) \tag{A36}$$

$$B_y = \mu_0(j\kappa h_x - \mu h_y) \tag{A37}$$

$$B_z = \mu_0 h_z \tag{A38}$$

This treatment ignores any loss mechanism in the spin resonance. Also we have not distinguished between the applied field and the internal field of the ferrite. These will not be equal in practice.

Index